THE COMPLETE GUIDE

To Creating
Your Own
Family
Tree

THE COMPLETE GUIDE
To Creating
Your Own
Family
Tree

PAUL BLAKE & AUDREY COLLINS

foulsham
LONDON • NEW YORK • TORONTO • SYDNEY

foulsham

The Publishing House, Bennetts Close, Cippenham,
Slough, Berkshire, SL1 5AP, England

Foulsham books can be found in all good bookshops or
direct from www.foulsham.com

ISBN 0-572-03160-2

Copyright © 2003 and 2006 Paul Blake and Audrey Collins

Photographs from the collection of Paul Blake on pages 6, 9, 11, 13, 15,
17, 18, 20, 22, 28, 31, 33, 34, 45, 47, 49, 50, 51, 52, 54, 57, 67, 69, 70,
71, 105, 106, 122, 125, 126, 127, 129, 133, 134, 139, 141, 143.
Photographs from the collection of Audrey Collins on pages 24, 26, 35,
56, 74, 76, 79, 81, 84, 95, 98, 103, 110, 112, 116, 117, 118.
Photographs copyright © Wendy Hobson on pages 36, 38, 41, 43, 48,
63, 64, 92, 100, 104, 136, 144, 146, 149, 150.
Photograph copyright © Chris Brewer on page 138.

35731743 6/07

Previously published as *Who Was Your Granny's Granny?*

Printed in Great Britain by Creative Print & Design (Wales), Ebbw Vale

Contents

From old documents and photographs to the latest internet sites, there's a vast range of information about your family waiting to be discovered.

Introduction

Genealogy – to give it its formal name – grips millions of people around the world. Once you start researching your family, who knows what may turn up? Few of us are related to the aristocracy or the famous, but understanding why and how an ancestor was sent to Australia for sheep stealing can bring history to life in a way that was rarely the case in the classroom.

So why does the past hold such fascination? There are many reasons to begin your own family's history, and these will influence the form your research takes. For example, you may wish to identify and contact living relatives, or there may be a family story you would like to prove, such as a connection with a famous person or event. If you have an unusual surname, you may want to trace its origin. Perhaps there is a branch of your family about whom you know little or nothing, because a parent or grandparent died young and contact was lost with the rest of the family.

The single greatest attraction, however, is probably to unlock the mystery of the past, to bring to life those enigmatic photographs of our grandparents or great-grandparents, to colour in the sepia tints in our imagination and find out what these people were really like and how they lived their lives. Where did they work? What was their home like? By delving into our family history, we can discover that the snappy 20s suit or voluminous Edwardian skirts cover people with characters just like our own!

Because, after all, our ancestors are a huge part of what makes *us*. While we all recognise the importance of our immediate family and our environment in shaping our characters, there is much in our own unique combinations of characteristics that comes to us from our inherited genes, passed down from one generation to another. Our ancestors give us our features, the colour and texture of our hair and skin and the shape of our face. We inherit the ability to move or think quickly, the probability of having twins, talents in the arts or sciences, music or mathematics. And we inherit behavioural traits, personality, generosity and meanness, kindness and cruelty. Abraham Lincoln may have said, 'I don't know who my grandfather was: I am much more concerned to know what his grandson will be', but possibly there isn't that much difference between the two.

It is a natural urge to understand who we are, and part of that understanding comes from where we come from. One of the major reasons family history has become so popular since the 1970s is that people feel that they have lost touch with their roots. Many families have moved from the areas where their ancestors lived for generations, and once close-knit families are now spread around the world. Knowing where we come from is a crucial element in our sense of identity. Alex Haley, author of the influential book *Roots*, wrote:

'In all of us there is a hunger, marrow deep, to know our heritage – to know who we are and where we come from. Without this enriching knowledge, there is a hollow yearning. No matter what our attainments in life, there is still a vacuum, an emptiness, and a most disquieting loneliness.'

In many ways genealogy is the ideal hobby. It is something that you can pick up or put down when it suits you. After all, your ancestors are not going to disappear. There is no pressure to trace everybody you are descended from – indeed it is nearly impossible. Most people only research one side of their family or a few ancestors who particularly interest them. And if one forebear is frustratingly elusive, well there are plenty of others out there for you to find. However, some researchers just want to tick off names with the bare minimum of information, while others, properly in our opinion, are more interested in finding out as much as they can about individuals. It's really all up to you.

The processes of searching, extracting and using information to build your own family tree can be very satisfying and even exciting at times. There really is nothing like the buzz you will get when, after months of searching, you finally find that elusive great-grandfather.

One of the great things about the pastime is how friendly and helpful most family historians are. If you get lost on your first visit to a record office, the chance is that somebody will be happy to point you in the right direction. Genealogists are a very sociable lot, and you will receive a warm welcome at your local family history society meeting or adult education class.

For some, family history leads them into totally new directions. It's an ideal way to learn about computing and the internet, while others become intrigued by aspects of local or military history and find that they devote more and more of their time to this subject. Whatever you do, and whatever direction you find yourself heading down, remember to enjoy yourself. It's a hobby after all!

Whether you want to build your own family tree from pure interest, or you have more specific reasons, this book will guide you step by step through the fascinating process of researching your family history. The place to start, naturally, is with what you know, so we'll show you how to collect and record the mass of information that is all around you – and you'll be surprised just how much there is to learn that way. You can then begin to trace back through the generations, learning and perfecting tried-and-tested research methods that you can then use to take your research wherever you want it to go.

Photographs can really help in learning about your recent ancestors.

The focus in this book is on English and Welsh ancestry because the other parts of the British Isles have different systems of registration and record-keeping. However, there's plenty of interest and relevance to those of us with ancestors from Scotland, Ireland, the Isle of Man and the Channel Islands, or even further afield.

And of course it is wonderful to be able to tell your children or grandchildren all about the life, work and loves of their granny's granny, who might well have witnessed events that otherwise would be dry and dusty entries in a history textbook.

How far back you will get with your family history research will depend on many factors. Not all records have survived for one thing – if indeed they were ever made in the first place. You may become 'stuck' at any point: this may be only a couple of generations back or in the sixteenth century. And probably 'stuck' is the wrong word anyway, although it is the one that is always used. There is always the possibility that the vital record or piece of information will come to light many months, or even years, after you have reached that initial impasse.

It is not the intention of this book to show you how to research your family back into the mists of time. We hope to show you how to start; to encourage you in your efforts and introduce you to the sources you will use in discovering your ancestors who lived during the nineteenth and twentieth centuries – the stepping-stones to earlier research. Possibly that is all you will ever want to do, but we hope not. Once on the ladder of family history research, many of you will find it difficult not to proceed further and further – as long as not too many rungs are missing.

CHAPTER 1

What's It All About?

Genealogy is nothing new. Some cultures have an oral tradition, so they can remember and recite lengthy family descents – just think of all those 'begats' in the Bible. In England, the College of Arms was established in the fifteenth century because newly rich families were using coats of arms to which they were not entitled. During the nineteenth century there was a steady trade in 'tracing' aristocratic ancestries for the expanding middle-classes. Many wanted to show that they had noble forebears, and there were always those willing to supply concocted pedigrees to prove their clients' claims.

For an aristocratic few, the College of Arms may hold your family's coat of arms.

Today, we are more interested in pursuing the truth, even if that results in 'ordinary' family trees. When Leo Blair, son of the British Prime Minister Tony Blair and his wife Cherie, was born in May 2000, *The Times* reported that 'Baby Blair's family tree reveals two murderers, a family of pro-slavery campaigners, a convict, a deserter, five drunks, 11 infamous actors – and a family secret.'

However, the claims through Cherie Booth's family now mostly appear to be false. The secret was that the Blair name had entered the family when James and Mary Blair fostered Tony Blair's father, also called Leo; his birth name was Parsons. We can't all be as lucky as young Leo Blair is with his family tree, but being ordinary to others does not mean that they are not extraordinary to us. An old English proverb says that 'He that has no fools, knaves or beggars in his family was begot by a flash of lightning'; so perhaps there is hope for all of us.

Whether we call it 'family history' or the somewhat more refined 'genealogy', we want to know who our ancestors were – and what they were. We want to know their names, and dates and places of birth, marriage and death. But we should also find out about their lives; how many brothers, sisters, aunts, uncles they had, where they were educated, what they did for a living, and so on. We want to know about them – after all, they made us what we are.

Names

In practice, the business of tracing a family history involves looking through lists of names – this is how we recognise our ancestors when we find them. Before the thirteenth century, people rarely had hereditary surnames: they were known just by a personal name or nickname. The Norman barons introduced surnames and the usage gradually spread. Most English families had adopted a name by 1400, although it was as late as the eighteenth century before the practice was widespread in parts of Wales. Even so, new surnames were still being formed much later and, of course, immigrants brought in new ones; over a generation or two these generally became anglicised, so are now often difficult to identify.

However, it is easy to place excessive importance on the family surname in the belief that knowing its meaning or origin may help in some way in tracing the family tree. Unfortunately this is rarely the case. As population increased and communication and travel became easier, it gradually became necessary to identify each person further: John the butcher, William the short, Henry from Sutton, Mary of the wood, Roger, son of Richard. Initially, these identifiers were changed or dropped at will but eventually they began to stick and were passed from one generation to another as inherited surnames. So trades and occupations, personal descriptions and nicknames, places of residence or origin, and fathers' names became fixed surnames: Fletcher and Smith, Redhead and Swift, Green and Pickering, and Wilkins and Johnson, for example.

Sometimes two different names can become one, being similar in sound even though different in origin. The fairly common name of Collins is an example of this; it comes from an Irish clan name and is also one of several English surnames derived from the personal name Nicolas. The surname Blake may seem fairly straightforward but there are three quoted derivations. Firstly as a variation of *Black*, itself being a descriptive name; secondly originating as the old English word *blac*, meaning pale; and lastly being a corruption of *Ap Lake*, a knight of the Round Table. The first definition is probably the most likely in this case, for the writer's family came from Wiltshire, where the surname Black is greatly outnumbered by Blake.

However, all this was a very long time ago, too far back to be of any practical use in researching family origins. Occasionally, a study of a particular surname may be of benefit when it is clear that it is largely found in a particular area or county – Saggers, Sworder and Barnard, for example, are all largely found on the Hertfordshire/Essex border. The distinguished genealogist George Pelling actually discovered that his ancestors came from Pelling, a small village in Sussex.

Victorian and Edwardian photographs were known as cartes de visite. If you are lucky, they may have a handwritten message on the back to identify the person in the picture.

In addition, it is important to realise that names change all the time, as different spellings are adopted either deliberately (Smythe for Smith) or accidentally, for example as the result of a bureaucratic error. Other people have adopted aliases or changed their names in order to inherit money in a will. If, during your research, an ancestor appears to disappear, one of the commonest reasons is that the surname changed, so it is worth checking common alternatives (for example, Heyward or Haywood for Hayward). This is particularly true for the period before the mid-eighteenth century when spelling had not been fixed. In Shakespeare's will, the clerk who drew up the document spelt the playwright's name in three different ways – none of which was used in his lifetime or even today.

Much less attention is paid by family historians to forenames, although these too can be a help (and a hindrance) in your research. It was not uncommon for children to be named after grandparents or a deceased aunt or uncle and even, on occasion, a deceased brother or sister. Middle names may indicate the mother's maiden name or alternatively be passed down the generations for no reason other than that it had always been done.

Relatively few Christian names were in general use until well into the nineteenth century. You may well find entries in a parish register for three or four babies with the same forename and surname christened within a few months of each other, which makes it almost impossible to work out from whom you are descended. This is the most common reason people abandon researching a particular line in their family tree. The use of unusual forenames, particularly those from the obscurer parts of the Bible, however, may indicate that the family were nonconformists, that is Quakers, Baptists and the like.

Change of name
As long as there is no intent to defraud or avoid any legal obligation and it is not for any criminal intent, you can use whatever surname you choose, without going through any formal process of change of name. In common law marriages, women often took their partner's names to give the appearance of marriage or of legitimacy for their children. Originally, wealthier members of society occasionally changed their names by a private Act of Parliament; this last happened in 1907. An alternative, from the seventeenth century,

These formal poses are typical of Victorian and Edwardian cartes de visite. Furniture details can sometimes give you clues to the date.

was a royal licence. After 1783 these were referred to the College of Arms and were normally advertised in the government's newspaper, the *London Gazette,* but this was very rare.

One of the more common methods of registering a name change is by deed poll – that is a deed involving only one party. This process applies only to British citizens living in Britain. Before 1903, these deeds could be enrolled (entered) in the Close Rolls of Chancery and from 1903 in the Enrolment Books of the Supreme Court of Judicature, but this was rarely done. Any records are now at the National Archives, indexed from 1851 by previous name. *An Index to Changes of Name 1760–1901,* edited by WPW Phillimore and EA Fry, lists many formal changes of name. From 1914, all deed poll enrolments were advertised in the *London Gazette.* After 1903, they could be entered in Supreme Court Enrolment Books and these are indexed under both names from 1905.

Between 1916 and 1971, non-British people were forbidden to change their names. The only exceptions were when a woman's name was changed at marriage or if the change was made by royal licence.

However, most people who wished to use a different surname either just did it without telling the authorities or made a statutory declaration before a magistrate (Justice of the Peace) or commissioner of oaths. There is no central record of these declarations. Some changes of name were referred to in newspapers, particularly *The Times,* so it may be worth checking the index to the paper.

Again there is no legal compulsion to use the forenames given at birth. Many people go through life using different first names. This is something you need to be aware of – Tig Vernon and Dorothy Vernon may be the same person, but Dorothy was always known as Tig (even sometimes in legal documents) after a childhood nickname, which was much preferred to a hated forename.

Legally, however, forenames given at baptism cannot be changed other than at confirmation, although they can be added to. The great statesman Winston Leonard Churchill, for example, added Spencer to his name. Names on birth certificates can be changed within 12 months of registration.

Cousins

The exact meaning of relationships, such as second cousin twice removed, is often confusing. Any relationship between two individuals refers back to their descent from a common ancestor. Therefore siblings (brothers and sisters) have the same parents – half-siblings only share one parent. First cousins have the same grandparents; second cousins have the same great-grandparents; and so on *ad infinitum.* 'Removed' describes how many generations from the actual cousin a person is. Therefore the child of a second cousin is 'second cousin once removed' and the grandchild of a first cousin is 'second cousin twice removed'.

Genetics

It is not surprising that the implications of genetic research have fascinated many family historians in recent years. The fact that genetics may help prove who our ancestors are, or indicate that disparate family groups with the same surname descend from the same pair of ancestors, is only part of this fascination. That we may now be able to know which physical characteristics have been passed on by long-dead ancestors is an interesting prospect. A geneticist recently claimed that 'knowing our genetic profiles can help us fulfil our desires to add lasting meaning to human life', although this is probably doubtful. Nevertheless, many family historians, particularly in the United States, are expanding their research to create family health histories that track important, disease-causing genes in their families. This research can only go back a few generations, as it is necessary to have actual examples of your forebear's DNA.

DNA is passed from one generation to another; some parts are almost unchanged from generation to generation while others suffer considerable deformation. As we have inherited our DNA from our ancestors, all our relatives, however distant, share with us a portion of this information. The closer the relationship, the more similar our DNA will be. It is therefore possible, in theory, to establish family links amongst individuals and families and even tribes and other indigenous groups. Distant cousins or those with the same surname can prove that they descend from the same male if they have the right DNA. It was this method that was used to show that President Thomas Jefferson had descendants by Sally Hemmings, one of his slaves: his own legitimate descendants sharing common DNA with their illegitimate cousins.

There are several firms advertising on the internet that will undertake DNA tests for a fee. However, using DNA tests to help trace your ancestry is not something that most people will be able to take advantage of – at least not at present. Where it

Details of clothing – or even styles of hair and beard – can help you to identify or date photographs.

is already becoming of use is in confirming, or otherwise, that families living in different parts of the country, or in different countries around the world and having the same or a similar surname, do have a common ancestor. In his book *The Daughters of Eve,* the scientist Bryan Sykes offers the thesis that all native Europeans originated from seven women who lived a few tens of thousands of years ago. But this is no help at all in identifying a missing ancestor in the nineteenth century. DNA testing may help narrow research, a form of localisation, but it is still a long way from proving who your ancestors were. This is an area of research where there may be significant strides forward in future years, but realistically it is never going to replace piecing together who one's ancestors were from old-fashioned records at archives and libraries.

A more recent development in the use of genealogical research has been in the building of medical family trees. These chart the age and cause of death of those on your family tree and may be useful if there is a suggestion of an inherited condition in your family. These can range from a serious disorder like Huntington's Chorea,

to a relatively harmless one such as colour-blindness. Backed by information on lifestyle (did they smoke, drink excessively or abuse drugs?), previous illnesses, and how long the individual had been suffering a terminal illness, it may be possible to analyse your own chances of suffering from any inherited illnesses.

This portrait of Charles Henry Blake, the author's grandfather, as a young boy is a fascinating heirloom to treasure and to bring alive the previous generations.

Medicine until fairly recently was quite an imprecise science, so the information on death certificates or in newspaper obituaries is often too general to indicate a risk of inherited diseases to members of your family. Heart disease, for example, may need to be further defined as arteriosclerosis, hypertension etc., and cancers can be of many different kinds, some inherited and some non-inherited. Mental illness was, and still is, often hidden by families and may be difficult to identify. The environment in which your ancestors lived or worked can be just as much a cause of disease. However, many inherited illnesses can be cured or alleviated if caught early enough, and knowledge of your ancestors' medical history may be the key to early detection.

Descendant tracing

A form of family history growing in popularity is descendant tracing. Many researchers, especially those outside Britain, are keen to discover living cousins 'back home'. Even if their own branch of the family emigrated back in the nineteenth century, they are keen to find cousins or other relatives still living in the United Kingdom. More recently, many families have become divided and, although they still live in the British Isles, contact has been lost. You may well receive a warm welcome from long-lost cousins, but you should also be wary as you could be resurrecting old family disputes.

Tracing descendants can be fraught with difficulties, although it is mostly the same records that will be used as those more widely used in genealogy. The biggest problem is often finding what names women adopted when they married.

A good place to start is the collections of electoral rolls and telephone numbers that can be purchased on CD-Rom, such as UK-Info. More about this service can be found at **www.192.com** or by ringing 020 7909 2192. This site claims to be the largest UK directory search service, with 13 million records on BT's Directory Enquiries database and more than 45 million people listed on the Voters' Register. Free registration allows you 20 searches per month, but there are also other registration packages for a fee that allow you unlimited numbers of searches and enhanced search facilities. There is also BT's Directory Enquiries website at **www.bt.com/directory-enquiries**. Available for purchase on CD-

You may be lucky enough to recognise a family heirloom, such as this brooch, being worn by a great grandmother.

Rom is UK Info Disk with over 60 million residential and business listings. This can be bought through the **www.192.com** website. There are many libraries, including the Society of Genealogists, which have copies. Most reference libraries also have sets of telephone directories, although these are often many years out of date. A recent court case about who can see electoral registers may restrict access in future. There are also a number of useful websites, such as Friends Reunited (**www. friendsreunited.co.uk**) or Missing You (**www. missing-you.net**).

More formally, the Traceline service, operated by the Office for National Statistics, will forward a letter from the enquirer to any living person, within certain stringent limitations, in England and Wales only. More information and details of the fee are available at **www.statistics.gov.uk/registration/traceline** or by writing to Traceline, PO Box 106, Southport PR2 2WA (tel: 0151 471 4811, e-mail: traceline@ons.gov.uk).

One-name studies

Another branch of genealogy is the one-name study, where a researcher attempts to track down everybody with the same surname. Such a study may concentrate on aspects such as geographical distribution of the name and the changes in that distribution over the centuries, or may attempt to reconstruct the genealogy of as many lines as possible bearing the name. A frequent aim is to identify a single original location of the name, especially if the name appears to derive from a place name. It is, of course, easier to choose uncommon names, so there is nobody chasing all the Smiths, although Smewing and Smitheman are being researched.

The Guild of One-name Studies has over 1,000 members who are researching particular surnames in depth. Over 7,000 surnames (and their variants) are now registered with the Guild. A list of these names, together with the contact details of the member concerned who is researching it, is available online at **www.one-name.org**. *A Register of One-name Studies* is published regularly, listing members' interests. Its address is: Guild of One-name Studies, The Registrar, c/o Box G, Society of Genealogists, 14 Charterhouse Buildings, Goswell Road, London EC1M 7BA.

Building up a picture

Your family history really begins to come alive when you can put your ancestors into context. Although nothing quite matches the thrill of finding a new, perhaps unexpected, piece of information about your family, your research is much more rewarding when you learn about the everyday lives of your ancestors and the times they lived in. With little effort you can discover what their everyday working lives may have been like, and the places where they lived, perhaps even their actual houses. You may not know what your ancestors looked like, but you can probably find contemporary pictures of the town or village where they lived and illustrations of the tools of their trade and the clothes they wore.

Background research into your ancestors' lives and times does not just illuminate and enrich your family history, it can help to make sense if it. To illustrate this, imagine you were researching the following real family: Henry Collins married Jane Carrick, and they had seven children at roughly two-year intervals, then an eighth child nearly ten years after the seventh one. This looks very odd, and you might wonder if you had missed the births of some children, or suspect that the youngest child was really the illegitimate offspring of an elder daughter being passed off as the child of her parents in the interests of respectability. Perhaps the

Seend.

Postcards, such as this one of Seend in Wiltshire, where Paul Blake's family lived in the nineteenth century, can be a valuable visual source of information about where and how your ancestors lived.

family moved abroad for a few years, or the parents separated for a while and were later reconciled. All of these are perfectly plausible solutions, but when you add the vital piece of information that the couple married in 1923, and the youngest child was born in 1947, another possibility emerges. It will be obvious that the missing years cover the period of the Second World War, so that the father was probably away on active service for the duration. In fact, Henry Collins was a prisoner of war in Italy for several years. However, once the War has passed from living memory, it might not occur to researchers to look for a record of the father's military service unless they had a basic knowledge of twentieth-century history. The Collins family illustrates the point that your ancestors did not exist in a vacuum; they were affected by the great (and small) changes that have always occurred in British society over the generations. If you take the trouble to find out about the background to their lives, you will not only enhance the results of the research you have already done, but your further research will be better directed as a result.

History is a fascinating subject, but when it is badly taught few things are more dreary. The lucky ones among us had inspired and inspirational history teachers at school but, for many, history lessons were boring and full of apparently meaningless dates. You should find it a much more enjoyable experience now, as there is a reason for wanting to learn – your family – and you can decide what you want to learn and when and how you do it.

If you lack even a basic knowledge of the outline of British and world history, you will need to buy or borrow a suitable book. There is a bewildering number of history books to be found in bookshops and libraries, which can provide background reading. If they seem too complicated, look in the children's section! School history websites also provide very useful background: try the excellent **www.spartacus.schoolnet.co.uk** or the National Archives' Learning Curve **http://learningcurve.pro.gov.uk**. There is also a range of monthly magazines on history and heritage. *History Today* and the *BBC History Magazine* are both attractively laid out and accessible, but still maintain a high standard of research. *Family History Monthly* also contains articles on social history written with the family historian in mind.

Almost every town, and most villages, have at least one published local history. There are also many books containing old photographs – three good series are published by Sutton, Phillimore and Tempus. County record offices, local study libraries, and family and local history societies may also publish books on local history. Their details are contained in the annual *Family and Local History Handbook*. Outside their locality they can be hard to come by, as they are usually on sale locally. However, any good bookseller should be able to order books for you provided they are in print and you know the title and author. Online alternatives are at **www.amazon.co.uk** or **www.historybookshop.com** – they are also useful places for seeing what is in print. Local studies libraries will probably have copies of local history books long out of print.

The most comprehensive local histories are the Victoria County Histories (VCH), which provides extremely detailed accounts of many places. The series began in 1899 and now consists of more than 200 large volumes. The aim is to cover every English county, although it is still by no means complete. Local reference libraries should have copies. Both the libraries of the Society of Genealogists and National Archives also have sets. More details about the project can be found at **www.englandspast.net**.

Old picture postcards are another good source of images depicting your family's past. The first ones were produced at the end of the nineteenth century. Pictures of churches are especially

ROYAL NAVAL HOSPITAL, GILLINGHAM, KENT.

Postcard fairs are good places to find pictures of the towns, and perhaps even the buildings, with which your family were associated.

popular, and you can probably find at least one for each of the churches where your family baptisms and marriages took place, but there are many others that may be of interest. If you had an ancestor in the navy, you can look for a picture of a ship on which he served, or simply any views of the towns or villages where your family lived. If you are lucky you may even find their place of work depicted, especially if it was a local landmark such as a post office or railway station. Tracking down cards is not difficult as there are specialist postcard fairs and there is a postcard stall or two at most family history fairs.

Museums are also a good way of finding out how your ancestors lived – not just in static displays but through programmes of special events, which might include re-enactments of historic events, or simply the re-creation of everyday life as it was in the past. Living museums, such as Beamish near Durham, or Ironbridge in Shropshire, allow you to visit shops and homes from a bygone age, staffed by attendants in costume who are playing people from the period. There are also more specialist museums dedicated to occupations. If your ancestors were in the navy, or worked in a naval dockyard, you will find much to interest you at Chatham and Portsmouth, no matter where they came from; and if they worked on the railways, there are excellent museums at Swindon and York. Many local and regional museums also have exhibits relating to local trades, and these are well worth seeking out. Northampton Museum, for example, recently opened a gallery dedicated to shoemaking – a recognition of the importance that the industry had in the town.

Sound and vision

History is a popular subject on TV and radio these days, and hardly a day goes by without programmes on one or more of the terrestrial TV channels, and several of the satellite and cable channels, some of which are entirely devoted to the subject. The history of the twentieth century is particularly well suited to television, as it is the first era for which there is a good supply of genuine moving pictures. The two World Wars are especially well served as there is always a high level of interest in them, but countless other events and themes have attracted the attention of documentary film-makers, and no doubt will continue to do so. If a picture is worth a thousand words, then the value of moving pictures is incalculable.

Second-hand bookshops are good sources of illustrated books, where you might find a picture of your town or village as it was when earlier generations of your family lived there, such as this delightful view of Dorking High Street in Surrey.

News and documentary material is, of course, of enormous interest, and is used extensively in many of these programmes. The British Film Institute is the repository for film archives, and arranges showings of features from the archives at the National Film Theatre in London. You can find more details on their website at **www.bfi.org.uk**, where there is also a catalogue of material available for hire. Another useful site is that of Pathé News, which many people will remember from visits to the cinema up to 1970, at **www.britishpathe.com**. Through the site you can preview 3,500 video copies of items that particularly interest you. Similar material can also be found in regular video, CD and DVD outlets, so there is no shortage of sound and vision material to provide an extra dimension to your family's past.

CHAPTER 2

Starting Out

Research takes time – the very last thing you should do is to rush it. Otherwise you might well miss out on a vital clue or element of the story. In some ways, a family historian is like a detective, piecing together clues based on painstaking research. Like all investigations, these clues lead to facts, and these facts almost inevitably include further clues indicating the next steps that need to be taken in the research process. Progressing from the known to the unknown is the golden rule of family history research. The more information and clues that you can gather before you start taking trips to record offices and libraries, the better. There is always the danger of undertaking unnecessary research and purchasing certificates you don't need, based on the wrong interpretation of the facts before you.

Begin with living memory

Family history really begins with events within living memory. Memory is a great recorder of truth, although don't forget that it can – and does – have lapses when flattery or fancy take over from fact.

Start by writing down all the basic information about yourself: full name, date and place of birth and, if applicable, any marriages and divorces. Then make a note of the less obvious: everywhere you have lived, with exact dates; the schools and colleges you attended, with dates and any qualifications you gained; where you have worked and when; your National Insurance number and any serious illnesses. Believe it or not, generations to come will find this interesting – after all, this is what you now want to know about your forebears. We've included a draft form at the end of the book to help you (see appendix A on page 151).

This summer holiday snap of Charles H, Emily and 'Bob' Blake is conveniently captioned with the location and date.

It's also important from the outset to keep accurate (and readable) notes of everything you discover. If you do not know the exact details about a person or event, either make sure that you find out or, if this is not possible, make a note that there is something that you cannot be certain about. You have started your family history research.

Before you even think about doing any research at all, you need to establish a few principles. The first of these is to start with the information you are sure of, and work backwards or outwards from that. There may be a story in your family that you are related to a famous – or infamous – person. It may be even be the reason that you became interested in tracing your family in the first place. It is very tempting to work on this interesting line and only later turn to proving the link with your own family. Resist the temptation. There is no such thing as a missing connection in a family tree. Until you have proved that two families are definitely related, you do not have one tree; you have two separate ones. You should always work from what you already know and can prove, and if you do find a link with the line you were hoping for, then that is a bonus and you can pursue it. If you spend time researching a family without being certain you are related, you can waste an awful lot of time and end up with a file marked 'ancestors I used to have', in the words of respected genealogist and writer Michael Gandy. Of course, the results will be of use to someone else, but unless your time and money are unlimited, it is best to stick to the facts that you know and work from there.

Never assume. If you find yourself saying or thinking 'I assume ...' stop and ask yourself why you don't know. If the reason you don't know is that you haven't looked for the evidence, go and look for it. If you can only assume something because you have not found any evidence, remember that it is only an assumption and could turn out to be wrong.

There is no such thing as a perfect source. Records were created by humans, and humans are fallible. Even the most carefully kept official records are prone to the occasional error (often in the spelling of surnames) and some (such as early parish registers) are not regarded as very reliable at all. If the records have been copied or indexed, then there are even more opportunities for errors and omissions.

One of the key sources you will use is a case in point. The indexes to births, marriages and deaths held at the Family Records Centre have been compiled from copies made by registrars and sent to the General Register Office, and it is known that not only are there some indexing errors but some events have been missed out altogether. The New Zealand researcher Mike Foster has carried out extensive research on this. Having said this, the error rate should not be overstated. Most people find what they are looking for most of the time, and you probably will, too. However, in a few cases these omissions or errors may be at the root of the problem, and it may be worth searching the indexes of the local register office where the event took place, if you know where this was.

Whom to research

As you start you should ask yourself exactly whose family you want to discover, and the answer will be entirely up to you. The choices are several, just the direct male line – that is your father or your mother's father, and his father and his father and so on; or the descent through the female members (your mother's mother, and her mother, and her mother); or all branches of the family (your two parents, four grandparents, eight great-grandparents, and so on). One strategy is to try to discover who your 16 great-great-great-grandparents were, your *seize quartiers*, and then decide which line or lines particularly interest you. If you get stuck on one you can then always turn to another. If you attempt to research every person on your family tree, by the beginning of the eighteenth century you could have 256 ancestors and a century earlier 2,048.

Another useful tip is to start with the ancestor with the most unusual surname, as it is undoubtedly true that they are much less difficult to research. It's easier to pick out unusual surnames in lists and indexes and you can be reasonably certain that the John Smewham in the parish register is your ancestor, but from which of the three John Smiths who were baptised in the same month are you descended? However, you should remember that because it is unusual, and clerks were unfamiliar with the spelling, it is likely to change over time.

Recording the present

But as you explore the past, spare a thought for the future, and think about telling your own story, creating your own personal and family archive for the future. You are recording the vital facts of your own life when you add events to your own family tree as they happen, but just think how much more this might mean to future generations if they know something about you. In Appendix A (see page 151), we have included a list of some of the questions that you should try to answer when writing your life history. No doubt others will occur when you get down to it. There may be courses at your local adult education centre about preparing life stories. In addition, several companies offer assistance in the process.

Family heirlooms
In the urge to begin your research it is very easy to overlook the wealth of information that is often to be found at home. Building up a full picture of your family as you go along is really as important as just discovering who your ancestors were. It is worth asking other family members, particularly older people, to see what they have. Remember always to keep anything you borrow in a safe place and return items in the same condition as they were handed to you.

Double-sided funeral cards were distributed to family and friends and can give a lot of detail about your ancestors.

In Affectionate Remembrance of

ANNIE,

The dearly Beloved Daughter of the late Francis Hartley,
of Hebburn Colliery,

Who died at 3, Elm Street, South Moor Colliery,

On Sunday, Feb. 14th, 1909,

AGED 23 YEARS.

Interment at Stanley, on Wednesday, Feb. 17th, at 3.30 p.m.
Service at the Wesleyan Church, Stanley, at 3 p.m.
Cortege to leave residence at 2.30.

Now is the time to start rummaging for family papers and memorabilia. What do you and your family have stored away? Go through the trunks in the attic and the boxes under the stairs. You are after anything: letters, medals, photographs, a family Bible, birthday books, funeral cards, old postcards, birth, marriage and death certificates, baptism certificates, school reports, newspaper cuttings, details of a family grave. You are after facts and you are after clues. Old photographs are wonderful but can they all be identified? Disregard nothing: it may be meaningless now but after a bit of investigation it may hold the vital piece of evidence you need. We've provided a checklist of the sort of things you might find in Appendix C (see page 169).

Always look after family heirlooms by keeping them out of direct sunlight and store them in a cool place away from potentially leaking pipes. You should also avoid handling them too often, as frequent touching may well damage them. If you are going to use original photographs or documents (such as marriage certificates) a lot in your research, then make copies.

Photographs
Amongst your family's memorabilia you may well find photographs of ancestors at various stages in their lives, as well as family groups, special events such as a wedding or christening, and snaps of the area in which people lived, perhaps showing bomb damage or a royal visit.

The earliest photographs date from the 1840s. Almost immediately, they became immensely popular. Specialist photographic studios sprang up around the country taking people's portraits. Slow exposure times meant that it was difficult to take shots without the subjects moving, which is why most early pictures look very posed.

The 1890s saw the first proper hand-held cameras, such as Kodak's Box Brownie, which were cheap enough to allow millions of people to take up the hobby. Picture postcards also became very popular. Colour film became more commonly used after the Second World War although it was available from before the First World War.

However, there can be some difficulties in using old photographs. In particular, it can be difficult to work out who appears in the picture, and when and where it was taken. There are several ways around this. The best is to ask elderly relations to see whether they can help. Changing dress fashions may also suggest an approximate date. During the World Wars there may be shots of family members in uniform: identifying regimental buttons and cap badges should tell you which unit they served with. Other sources, such as birth certificates, may provide a clue, if you know somebody was born or married at a certain time. And, of course, there may well be something on the back, such as the name and address of the studio where the photograph was taken. Local directories may give an idea when a studio was in operation. Lastly, you may be able to guess an approximate age. However, before the Second World War, people in general aged much quicker, so by today's standards even fairly young people can look old.

Talking to relatives
Talking to relations who actually knew your direct ancestors, or have stories to tell about them, is something that can never be replaced by historic records. By asking questions, particularly of your older relatives, you may get some more vital clues. You should not risk complete reliance on family stories, but you should not ignore them either; just treat them with caution. Nor should you only speak to older relatives: grandparents often have more time to spend with their grandchildren than they did with their own children when they were young, so tales of their childhood and family may skip a generation.

It is unlikely that you will know all your living relatives. Certainly you are unlikely to be fully acquainted with all your great-uncles and aunts, second cousins and the more distant relations. You may possibly know a name or two but not too much more. However, it is possible

Charles H Blake's Past President and Honours medals of the Retail Fruit Trade Federation Limited.

The mount surround tells us that this cabinet photograph of an immigrant was taken in Sarajevo.

that these are the very family members who will hold the vital clues you will need to make progress in your investigations.

How you make contact is relatively unimportant although there is a lot to be said in favour of writing, especially to those you do not know too well. One way to unearth the information you are after is to send them a copy of the information that you already have, preferably in the form of a simple family tree. Most people can understand these, if it is not made too complicated, whereas, if you constantly refer to great-grandmother this or second cousin that, it is easy to become confused. Seeing an illustration of their family's tree is more likely to get people thinking than a detailed written report. This is especially the case if you have managed to get some detail or other wrong. It has been suggested that you should include some deliberate mistakes just to get a reaction!

You can also include a simple questionnaire laying out the questions you would like answered. We've included a sample one in Appendix A (see page 151). These questions can be quite specific, being about names, dates or places, perhaps of a birth or a marriage. You can also ask what school someone went to, or if they served in the armed forces, or what they did for a living. Other questions can be more general, enquiring about any photographs, a family Bible, letters, stories about the family and so forth. And remember, you can always go back with further queries, so don't try to get too much into your initial enquiry or you might put the relative off.

It is also important that you make sure that whoever you are contacting knows who you are. If you know very little about them, then the reverse is almost certainly the case too. And reassure them from the outset that the research that you are undertaking is just for your and the current family's own benefit, building a bigger and better picture of the family. It is not part of some scam to do them out of their inheritance. Many people are, quite understandably, protective of their own history and need to be assured that what you are doing is not going to undermine that. Accounts from relatives may contradict each other, or be at variance with your own memory. This need not be a problem, provided that you keep a note of where each piece of information came from, and check everything whenever you can.

During your research, it may become clear how a story came about, even if it is not true. A 'typical' family legend is that you are related to some famous person, such as Horatio Nelson. This could be true, but remembering that a number of nineteenth-century Nelson families named a son after the great naval hero, your Horatio may be a bootmaker in Stepney, not an Admiral of the Fleet.

This invoice does not only include names, but tells us how much it cost to have the family cottage decorated in 1909.

You can ask your relatives if they have any family photographs, but make sure you identify the people if you can, such as this grandmother with her two daughters and youngest grandson. Note the detail from incidental items such as the newspaper.

Alternatively, members of the family might claim descent from the Duke of Marlborough and, on investigation, you find that an ancestor ran a pub of that name. Then there is the apocryphal tale of the ancestor who died at Waterloo, who turned out to have broken his neck falling down a flight of stairs at Waterloo station. On the other hand, that seemingly fanciful tale might even turn out to be true after all.

Other information may turn out to be almost true, but not quite. A common example concerns dates of birth. Relatives may insist that your grandfather was born on 12 March 1886, but you cannot find this name indexed for that date. The solution is often to look a year or two either side, when you might find he was actually born on 12 March 1885. Then again, the date of birth may occasionally be found to be exactly a week out: possibly because the registrar misinterpreted 'she was born last Wednesday', or it was a deliberate false statement in order to avoid having to pay for a late registration. Sometimes a story is true, but has been credited to the wrong relative, so if you find that your great-grandfather was a coalminer, and not a ship's captain as you were told, try looking to find out if another relative went to sea instead.

Reviewing the situation

At this point you may feel discouraged if you have no such treasures and no older relatives, or only unco-operative ones. Don't worry. You can start with nothing more than your own birth certificate and have as much success as anyone; it just means you do not have the benefit of any shortcuts.

The chances, however, are that you will have many bits of information which you will have to go through to carefully work out how they all fit together. In particular, you will have to separate this information into what is actual evidence (such as a marriage certificate) and what is only circumstantial, such as the family tradition that an ancestor fought at Waterloo. You will also need to consider whether you really know as much as you should about those relations. Are there, for example, any missing details such as dates of marriage or death?

It may be a good idea to prepare a chart or form for each family member where you can note down all definite information you have, possible truths or half-truths, and where the major gaps are. At the very least you should have birth, marriage and death dates for your parents, grandparents and so on, together with some idea of their occupations and where they lived.

Who else is out there?

With hundreds of thousands of family historians around the world, there is always the possibility that someone somewhere is looking for some or all of the same forebears as you are, perhaps a distant cousin of whom you know nothing. Unfortunately there is no one place that is going to give you a list of all the families currently being researched. However, there are libraries, publications and websites that between them will provide the information you require. It is something you'll need to check fairly frequently, as the information is updated regularly. If you discover somebody else researching your line, it can be a huge shock, although in fact it may turn out to be very advantageous. We all like to think that we are the first, but the mutual help and knowledge that you can share with fellow researchers is often part of what makes family history so rewarding. And, who knows, they may have that vital clue that allows you to complete the missing gap in your research.

Gradually, you will be able to build up a real picture of your family – such as where they spent their family holidays. Look at background details to help you define the location.

Never assume that somebody else's research is correct. Just because something is in print it does not mean it is necessarily accurate. This isn't meant to imply that genealogists in the past deliberately lied, although occasionally they did. Nevertheless, even with the best of intentions mistakes could (and still can) be made. So be very careful and wherever possible check absolutely everything for yourself.

Over the centuries, many individuals have researched their own family histories. Other families (generally the well-to-do) may have been described by local antiquaries and historians, or possibly written about as the result of a court case over inheritance or to determine legitimacy. These family pedigrees may cover many generations or a very few; may be very detailed or just in outline; they may have been published in several volumes or only survive on the back of a sheet of wallpaper.

Many of the earlier published pedigrees are listed in a number of reference works. *The Genealogist's Guide,* by GW Marshall (published in 1903) notes those pedigrees which included three generations in the male line published before 1900. J Whitmore's *The Genealogical Guide* (1953) covers more recent pedigrees published between 1900 and 1950. *The Genealogist's Guide,* by G Barrow (1977) indexes pedigrees and family histories published from 1950 to 1977. *A Catalogue of British Family Histories,* by T Thompson (1980) lists those pedigrees published between 1977 and 1980. These volumes, especially Marshall and Whitmore, tend to cover only the upper echelons of society and not ordinary families.

Burke's Peerage and Baronetage (from 1826), *Burke's Landed Gentry* and *Debrett's Peerage* (started in 1769 as the *New Register*) also contain many pedigrees. Again, as the names suggest, they cover the aristocracy, although it is surprising how often noble families come from humble origins and how quickly their descendants return to being just ordinary folk. In America, the Genealogical Publishing Company (GPC) has published many books of pedigrees of early settlers, the vast majority of whom came from the British Isles.

The Society of Genealogists (for more details see below) also has a substantial number of family histories, often published privately by family historians based on their researches. Copies may sometimes be found in local libraries and record offices. It is always worth enquiring at libraries near where your family came from to see whether something has been written that refers to them. All published books should appear in the catalogue of the British Library, which can be searched online at **www.bl.uk**.

In Salt Lake City, the massive Family History Library has more than 70,000 biography and family history volumes. It is possible to search the catalogue of the Library either online at **www.familysearch.org** or at any Latter-day Saints (Mormon) family history centre. If your search reveals a published genealogy, and it has been microfilmed, then you can order a copy of the film, for a small fee, to read at your local family history centre. Over the years, *The Genealogists' Magazine* (first published by the Society of Genealogists (SoG) in 1925) has included references to thousands of different families. There is an index to surnames that appeared in the journal up to 1996 on the Society's website **www.sog.org.uk**.

Sometimes, when there isn't enough material to fill a book, a researcher may have written up the family history and submitted it to a genealogical journal. The *Periodical Source Index (PERSI)* is a comprehensive subject index covering genealogy and local history periodicals since 1800. More than 1.1 million entries from nearly

6,000 titles are included. *PERSI* is searchable by surname and will refer to the title of the article and publication. The index was created by Allen County Public Library, Fort Wayne, Indiana, and therefore includes mostly American material. There is, nevertheless, much British-sourced information that is definitely worth checking. The index is available online through the **www.ancestry.com** website, and the SoG and some major libraries have copies.

In Britain, *Family History News and Digest,* published by the Federation of Family History Societies twice a year, includes a summary of the contents of the publications of local family history societies, including articles about people's research. The Federation also publishes a series of county bibliographies by Stuart A Raymond, which list books and publications available locally.

The *Genealogical Research Directory* (GRD) is the largest surname queries listing of its kind. It has been published annually in book form since 1981 and contains entries from around the world. The 2002 edition contained 130,000 entries from over 5,400 contributors. Every year, contributors supply lists of the family names that they are researching, together with information on place and time period. These are then published in alphabetical order with a reference to the name and address of the submitter. Contributors also pay a fee (somewhere around £20) for a basic 15 entries and a copy of the directory. The information in each edition is not cumulative, so it is always a good idea to try to look in the last three or four editions for the names in which you are interested. Non-contributors can also buy the directory and it is available in most family history society libraries and many reference libraries, as well as at the Society of Genealogists. The 2002 and subsequent editions are also available on CD-Rom. Also available on two CD-Roms only are cumulative editions of the GRD, between 1990 and 1999 (600,000 entries), and between 2000 and 2002 (225,000 entries). Further information is available from their website at **http://members.ozemail.com.au/~grdxxx**.

A similar publication is *The British Isles Genealogical Register (The Big R),* which is published irregularly by the Federation of Family History Societies. The latest edition was published in 2000 with nearly 400,000 entries. It is available on CD-Rom or microfiche. In addition most family history societies publish lists of names being researched by their own members, either in their journal or in a separate publication. In addition the commercial genealogical magazines include sections advertising names being researched, and readers are encouraged to submit entries for free.

For people with access to the internet, it is well worth typing the surnames you are researching into a search engine to see what it comes up with. Thousands of researchers (particularly in America) are uploading their genealogical files to pedigree-linked databases where it is now possible to find families linked for perhaps four, five or more generations. Results are unpredictable, and it is essential to check any information you find, but this approach is certainly worth a try. Surname mailing lists – the online equivalents to the *Genealogical Research Directory* and *The Big R* – are becoming more common, and it is again worth checking to see if any exist for your name interests, although inevitably they are likely to be dominated by American researchers. Many of these are run by Rootsweb (**www.rootsweb.com**), where there is a surname list of more than 700,000 entries, and **www.geneforum.genealogy.com** hosts forums for over 160,000 surnames. Plus there are 65,000 message boards for surnames at **www.familyhistory.com**.

If you have family photographs such as this delightful wedding group of brothers and friends, try to identify as many of the group as possible by talking to your elderly relatives.

With luck, you will have made contact with at least one other researcher who is researching the same line as you. In any initial letter or e-mail, explain what you are looking for and, of course, always emphasise that you are happy to exchange information – the more you share, the more you receive. Certainly in the early days, don't be tempted to send too much information in one go – wait until you have received something in return before revealing everything you know. If you are writing, enclose a stamped self-addressed envelope, together with, if you are writing abroad, two or three International Reply Coupons (IRC). These can be bought at any post office.

Sharing your research

Preserving and presenting your research is obviously worthwhile, having made the effort to collect it in the first place, and you may want to share it with anyone who has an interest in the family. This can be done in a number of ways. You can submit entries to directories such as the *Genealogical Research Directory* and *The Big R*, where other researchers will see reference to it. You can also contribute to one of the websites. And, of course, you can set up your own website. It's pretty simple to do and there are sites on the internet or provided by your internet service provider that can help you. Free software to build simple web pages may come bundled with your genealogical software or can often be found given away with computer magazines. The more recent versions of Microsoft Office also allow you to build simple sites.

Traditionalists can also publish the written version of their family history in book form, and distribute copies among the family. You might decide to wait until you have finished researching your family history before you write it up. However, if you wait to finish researching before you start writing, you will never get around to it because there will always be just one more piece of research to do. If you keep good records as you go along, you can produce a written up version when you have gathered a reasonable amount of information. You can always add to it later as your research progresses, and you may find that receiving a copy of their genealogy encourages family members to provide more information for you.

Consulting someone who knows about cars could help you date this picture and therefore identify the little girl.

Publishing books is much less complicated than it sounds. Even ordinary word processors can easily produce A4 or A5 booklets. You can then physically produce the booklets yourself, or have them done by a printer. Printing used to be a very expensive option, and not economic for short runs, but the advent of digital printing has changed this. Digital printing is rather like a very sophisticated kind of photocopying, where hard copy of the pages are fed into the printer, and out of the other end come the finished softback books, complete with covers, all neatly stapled together. Printers who provide this service advertise in the family history press, or you could ask your local printer, or even an ordinary high street photocopy shop to see what they have to offer. You can find out more about the subject in John Titford's *Writing and Publishing Your Family History*.

As well as family members, you should give copies to the local studies library or record office of the area where the family lived, as well as to the Society of Genealogists Library, so that other family historians can use your research. If you publish your book, you are required to send copies to the British Library and the five other deposit libraries in the British Isles.

Family history societies

Following the huge rise in interest in family history in the 1960s and 70s, many local societies dedicated to the encouragement of the hobby were formed. The number of individuals who now belong to one or more societies runs into many tens of thousands. Local societies have now been joined by societies with some special interest, such as the Anglo–German FHS, the Catholic FHS, the Guild of One-name Studies and the Romany and Traveller FHS. There are also a number of one-name societies, whose members are researching a particular surname. A list of societies can be found at **www.genhomepage.com/societies.html**.

Should you join your local family history society? The answer is an emphatic yes, even if your ancestral home is many miles away from where you live now. Most organise monthly meetings with speakers on different subjects and some provide special sessions for beginners. Most societies produce a quarterly magazine, which includes articles on local records and history, and index and publish transcripts of local records, such as parish registers and surname indexes to the census. Some societies now have their own library or research room where members can visit and undertake research with the material held there. Membership is usually very reasonable – about £10 a year.

It is also a good idea to join the societies for the districts in which your ancestors once lived, particularly if they were there for more than a couple of generations. Their members may be able to help if you find it difficult to visit the ancestral home, for example by visiting the churchyard to read your grandfather's gravestone for you.

You can find out which is the nearest society on the website of the Federation of Family History Societies at **www.ffhs.org.uk** or by asking at your local library.

Society of Genealogists

The Society of Genealogists was founded in 1911 'to promote and encourage the study of genealogy and heraldry'. It has over 15,000 members around the world. The Society's library is by far the largest genealogical library in Europe. It is open to non-members (for a fee). In it you will find the country's largest collection of parish register transcripts and indexes, together with many local histories, copies of monumental inscriptions, poll books, trade

Family histories shelves at the Society of Genealogists give a clue as to the amount of fascinating information waiting to be discovered.

directories and census indexes. There are also copies of the indexes to births, marriages and deaths for England and Wales (1837–1920), for Scotland (1855–1920) and for many Britons overseas. The Society has a large collection of miscellaneous manuscripts and typescript family histories, not to be found elsewhere, as well as indexes on CD-Rom and the internet. The Society's website **www.sog.org.uk** is very informative and includes a list of its parish register holdings.

One of the Society's treasures is a vast collection of pedigree rolls of all shapes, sizes and dates. In addition, members are encouraged to complete birth briefs, which show their 16 great-great-grandparents. Over the years, members and others have donated their unwanted or completed research in the hope that one day it will be of some use to a researcher. Once you've completed your research you might also consider giving it to the Society. The larger donations form the Special Collections. However, it is the Document Collection that so often contains individual gems. It is housed in several hundred boxes, which are largely arranged by surname (11,000 of them in total). The envelopes may contain a complete pedigree, rough notes, extracts from deeds or wills – just about anything.

The Society also runs a very full lecture programme and other courses for family historians. In addition, the Society publishes a number of books, including the well-known *My ancestor was* series. The Library is open Tuesday, Wednesday, Friday and Saturday from 10 am to 6 pm; and Thursday from 10 am to 8 pm.

Family history centres

Often known as the Mormons, members of the Church of Jesus Christ of the Latter-day Saints are expected to trace their family trees in order posthumously to baptise their ancestors. Over the past 150 years, they have collected a vast amount of genealogical information, virtually all of which is available to be used by those who are not members of the Church, for little or no charge. The most important of these resources is the International Genealogical Index, which lists hundreds of millions of births, baptisms and marriages (but few deaths) taken from parish registers and other records from around the world. This can be viewed on their website which is at **www.familysearch.org**.

Master copies of the microfilmed and fiched records – about 2.5 million items – are stored in the Granite Mountain Records Vault, an enormous facility excavated out of the mountains south-east of Salt Lake City in Utah.

In addition to the main Family History Library in Salt Lake City, there are hundreds of branch libraries, or family history centres, around the world. There are a hundred or so centres in the British Isles, the main one being the Hyde Park Centre opposite the Science Museum in London. Details of these centres can be found on the familysearch website and are listed in the *Family and Local History Handbook*. This site also includes the *Family History Library Catalogue* describing the material held in Salt Lake City. Most items can be ordered, for a minimal charge, to view at any of the local family history centres.

Learning more

Some family history societies run their own classes teaching people about the family history basics, but the majority are organised by a local authority or the WEA (Workers Educational Association). These classes are highly recommended for beginners to family history. Some courses can take place over a few days whilst others may last for 6, 12 or even 20 sessions. There are also intermediate and advanced courses for those who want to extend their knowledge. Your local authority or family history society will be able to tell you what is available in your area. Most classes are held on weekday evenings but some take place in the daytime or at weekends. It's also a good way of meeting fellow enthusiasts and sharing your research problems among like-minded people.

Papers from the Document Collection at the Society of Genealogists range from rough notes to formal deeds or wills.

Conferences and fairs

Conferences, lasting a couple of days or longer are a regular feature in the family history world. Many are organised by local family history societies or regional groups, sometimes with a particular theme. There are normally two major conferences each year organised by the Federation of Family History Societies or its member societies, which are attended by several hundred people. Quite apart from the formal proceedings, many ideas are exchanged during informal discussion and social events.

This football team photograph could hardly be easier to date! Your grandfather may be able to fill in the details of his school and his team-mates.

Many family history societies now hold open days, sometimes in conjunction with their annual general meeting. At these you can learn about the host society and usually neighbouring societies, which often attend with their own stalls. You will probably be able to use their research collections or buy from the bookstalls. There are often talks taking place at these events too.

There are also numerous family history fairs. The largest is the one organised over the early May Bank Holiday weekend by the Society of Genealogists at the Royal Horticultural Society Halls in London. All these fairs include stands from local family history societies, together with stalls demonstrating and selling computer software, offering new and second-hand books, and local record offices providing advice to visitors. A full list of known family history fairs, events and activities can be found online at **http://users.ox.ac.uk/~malcolm/genuki/Geneva**. Family history magazines, particularly *Family History Monthly*, also list forthcoming fairs.

Family history magazines

There are currently three magazines dedicated to family history available on the bookstalls. These are *Family History Monthly*, *Family Tree* and *Practical Family History*. They all include articles on

Tel. : KENSINGTON 4842-3

C. H. BLAKE,

ESTABLISHED 1880

FLORIST

FRUITERER & GREENGROCER

FLORAL DECORATIONS for Weddings, Dinners, Receptions, Dances and other functions   :   :

WREATHS   ON   SHORTEST   NOTICE

Fresh Fruit and Vegetables, Salads, &c., daily in Season

78 & 80 KING'S ROAD, S.W.3

(Opposite " Duke of York's " H.Q.)

and 79 Royal Hospital Road

KING'S ROAD—continued.
30 & 32 Midland Bank Ltd (R. H. White, mngr)
... *here are Cadogan gdns* ...
34 Lilley & Skinner Ltd. boot mkrs   .
36 Grant Jn. butcher
38, 40, 42, 44, 46 & 52 Smith Sidney (Chelsea) Ltd. genl. drapers
38A, Sieber & Selby, furriers
42, 44, 46, 52 & 38 & 40 Smith Sidney (Chelsea) Ltd. genl. drapers
44 **BARRATT W. & CO. LTD.** footwear specialists
46 French Cleaning & Dyeing Co. Ltd. (receiving office)
46A, Clark Wltr. Fell
46A, Mezadour   Madame Noemi, court dressma
46A, Hodson Miss
52 Smith Sidney (Chelsea) Ltd. milliners
54 Vines Ltd. fruitrs
56 & 58 Sainsbury J. Ltd. provsn, mers

60-62 Woolworth F. W. & Co. Ltd. stores
64 & 100 Wagstaff Herbt. Hy. gentlemen's outfitter. See advertisement
64A, Kirkpatrick Colin
66 **COBB GEORGE**, butcher. Tel. No. Kensington 6534
68 to 70 Freeman, Hardy & Willis Ltd. boot mkrs
68 to 70 Felice (Mrs. P. Gossage), lampshades
70A, Heron-Maxwell Miss
... *here is Blacklands ter* ...
72 The   Colville   tavern (Pioneer Catering Co, Ltd)
...... *here is Lincoln st* ......
74 Legg Charles S. ladies' outfitter
74 Harrison Miss Kathleen
74 Carey Miss
76 Allworthy, jeweller
78 Blake   Charles Henry, greengrocer. See advertisement
80 Blake   Charles Henry, florist. See advert

80A, Rubin Mrs
80A, Gladstone-Davies Miss
82 Taylors Cash Chemists (London) Ltd
82 Staples Ltd. dentists
82 Rowe Wm. Hy
84 Goodbody Alfd.Geo.dentst
84 Smith A. J. & Co. Limited, wine merchants
86 Salmon   &   Gluckstein Limited, tobacconists
88 Northampton Shoe Renovators
90 Andrews A.& Co.butchers
92, 94 & 96 Boots Cash Chemists (Southern)Ltd
98 Lipton Lim. tea merchnts
100 & 64 Wagstaff Herbert Henry, gentlemen's outfitter. See advertisement
102, 104 & 106 Wakeford Brothers Ltd. drapers
108 Pritchard T. baker
...... *here is Anderson st* ......
110 International Tea Co's. Stores Ltd. wine mers
110 Church Willie
112 Parker Arthur, draper

An advertisement in Kelly's Directory *of Chelsea 1934 tells us more about Charles Blake's shop on King's Road.*

Business as usual at Charles Blake's fruit and vegetable shop during the Second World War.

a variety of subjects, help and advice pages and news about what is happening in the family history world. All carry advertising and this is an excellent way of discovering what new books, computer software and indexes have become available. Also available is the bi-monthly *Ancestors,* which is published by the National Archives. Currently this is only available by subscription or in the NA bookshops at Kew and the Family Records Centre.

CHAPTER 3

Conducting Research

In order to undertake research you will have to visit record offices, libraries and similar places to use the wealth of information available there to unlock the mysteries of your ancestors' lives. Not so long ago, visiting most record offices was a daunting experience for even experienced genealogists. Now, part of the delight of family history is being able to not only see, touch and use original documents hundreds of years old, but also to be able to do so in archives and libraries that are positively welcoming.

The chances are that, at the beginning of your research, you will only handle copies rather than the originals themselves. Copying was done to protect fragile documents, but it did mean that microform (microfilm or microfiche) copies could be distributed

When undertaking research at libraries and record offices, you may have to order up the material you wish to research, so you need to do your homework before planning a trip.

widely. It is only recently that digitised images of the records themselves have become available over the internet or on CD-Rom. The 1901 Census Returns of England and Wales is one of the largest collections available in this form (at its website **www.census.pro.gov.uk**). This now means that we are beginning to be able to use at home, records that were previously only available in archives, perhaps half way around the world.

There are two main differences between record offices and libraries. Firstly, in a library you will find material on particular subjects (such as genealogy or gardening) kept together; whereas in a record office, material created or owned by a particular body (such as the War Office or the Midland Railway) is kept intact. This is rarely a problem as there are usually good finding aids allowing you to access the information wherever it is kept. The second difference is that in a library, most books are kept on open shelves so you can simply help yourself, whereas in a record office most material is kept locked away in strong-rooms and has to be ordered up before it can be investigated.

Before you visit an archive you should phone to check that they have the items you are looking for and to book a seat if necessary. You should also take with you a notebook and a pencil or two – as pens are not allowed into the reading room because of the damage

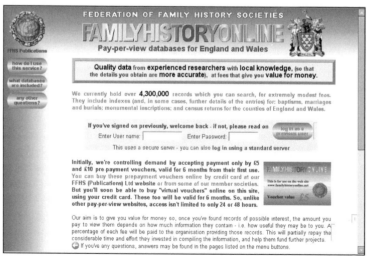

More and more research can now be done online, through sites such as the Federation of Family History Societies FamilyHistoryOnline website.

they can do to priceless documents. A pound coin for lockers and a packed lunch are also good ideas.

Almost every record office, and many local studies libraries, have their own website with details about their services. They also appear in *Yellow Pages*. Some record offices issue their own reader's ticket, although most belong to the County Archive Research Network (CARN) where one card issued at a participating office is valid at the others. You'll need to take some form of identification with you when you apply for a ticket, and possibly a passport photograph as well.

In order to maximise your time at a record office you'll need to pre-plan your visit. Firstly, be quite clear in your own mind what it is you intend to do when you get there – make a list. Always phone before making your visit. It's sensible to check that they have what you want to look at – books and records do go off for rebinding and conservation. You need to make sure the place is open when you intend to visit and isn't closed for the annual stock-take, because of shortage of staff, or the roof has blown off (that has happened!). You may have to make an appointment, and people have been turned away because one of the smaller record offices was full – not much fun if you have travelled a considerable distance. You may be required to book a microfilm or fiche reader, or a computer terminal.

The way a particular office arranges its holdings can vary greatly. It can take a little time to understand the system being used, so don't be afraid to ask staff for their help – tell them this is your first visit. Their indexes and catalogues will probably need explaining, as will the way documents are ordered up. Always ask what personal name and place indexes they have – you may find important references in minutes if you are lucky.

The finding aids for the documents held by a record office can be of several different types, so perhaps here a few definitions are in order. A catalogue is a list (or a set of cards), systematically or methodically arranged, alphabetically or in some other order. It also often has brief particulars, either descriptive or aiding identification by locality, date or in some other way. An index is a list – arranged alphabetically, numerically or by some other system – of references to people, places or subjects mentioned in the book or record, with an indication as to where they occur. A calendar is a list or register of documents for a specific period, arranged

The Access to Archives (A2A) website aims to make most local record indexes and catalogues available online.

chronologically, with a short summary of the contents of each, so as to serve as an index to them. Increasingly these differences are fading away as finding aids are computerised. The most important of these new finding aids is the Access to Archives project which aims to make the vast majority of local record office indexes and catalogues available online at **www.a2a.pro.gov.uk**.

There are a few basic rules that apply to every record office you will visit. No food, drink or smoking is allowed in the search room and graphite pencils only will be permitted. Outdoor clothes, bags and mobile phones will all probably be banned. There are usually lockers provided for you to use, together with somewhere to eat the snack lunch you have brought with you. Laptop computers and dictaphones are usually allowed in the search room, but do ask first. It goes without saying, but the records you are using are unique and may be centuries old. Treat them with the due care they deserve. You may well be asked to use some form of bookrest so as not to break the spine of a volume. Keep your fingers off the face of the page and be ready to wear special gloves if asked to do so. Quite rightly, the survival of the record is always more important than your need to see it.

Occasionally the records you want to look at may not be available, usually because they are in too poor a condition to be produced. The other reason is that they have not yet been released to the public, often because they contain sensitive personal information. Personal files, for example, are normally closed for 75 or 100 years. Sometimes you can get access if you can prove that you are related to the individual you seek.

Many record offices or specialist libraries offer a paid research service for people who can't visit in person. Fees vary but are seldom low. Alternatively, the office may be able to supply a list of researchers who can undertake research for you for a fee – they will rarely recommend any particular researcher. The Association of Genealogists and Researchers in Archives (AGRA) has members all around the country. Details, including a list of members available for research, can be found on its website **www.agra.org.uk** or a list is available from 29 Badgers Close, Horsham, West Sussex RH12 5RU. The various genealogical magazines also contain advertisements from professional researchers.

There are several guides to record offices and libraries, providing addresses and perhaps an idea of what is available. We provide a list of the most important centres on pages 185–187. *Record Offices: How to Find Them* by J Gibson and P Peskett includes details of nearly all county and diocesan record offices and archive departments in England and Wales, together with repositories in Edinburgh; with a sketch map, address and contact details. More comprehensive, but without the benefit of the maps, is Ian Mortimer's *Record Repositories in Great Britain*. Many professional bodies and national societies also have their own libraries and collections of records. Such places are included in *British Archives* by Janet Foster and Julia Sheppard. This is the most comprehensive guide to the wealth of archives in Britain describing well over 1,200 separate archives, with details of how you can access them: your local reference library should have a copy. The annual *Family and Local History Handbook* includes a very comprehensive listing of libraries, record offices, archives and museums, and has the advantage of being updated each year. All county record offices and most smaller, more specialist, archives have a website, which may just provide basic information about the holdings and how to use them, but many are much more comprehensive. Links to all of them can be found at **www.hmc.gov.uk/archon**.

Useful books for library sources are *Libraries in the United Kingdom and Republic of Ireland* and *The ASLIB Directory of Information Sources in the United Kingdom*. On the internet, a

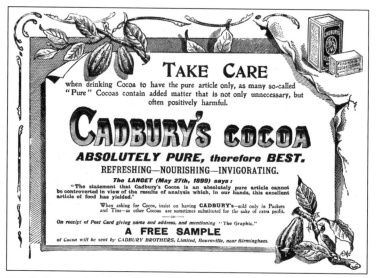

This Cadbury's advert from a newspaper of 1900 shows that some of the brand names were just as familiar to our ancestors as they are today.

directory of family history resources held in public libraries throughout Britain and Ireland is available at **www.familia.org.uk**. London requires particular mention and *London Local Archives: A Directory of Local Authority Record Offices and Libraries* is an essential guide. Terry and Shirley Wise describe regimental museums in *A Guide to Military Museums and Other Places of Military Interest.*

National Archives

The most important British archive is the National Archives at Kew (formerly the Public Record Office), which houses records created by the actions of central government and of the courts of law of England and Wales. The records span an unbroken period from the Domesday Book to the latest government papers to be released to the public, which are generally 30 years old. There are considerable numbers of records of interest to family historians, and it is little surprise that genealogists make up over two-thirds of the visitors to the Archives. Of particular note are records relating to the armed services, railways, immigration and emigration, taxation, civil servants and the Metropolitan Police.

Anyone aged 14 or over can use the National Archives. You do not need any special qualifications or referees, or indeed need to make an appointment in advance. Access is free. Experts are on hand to help, although they cannot do detailed research for you. The Archives is open Monday to Saturday, roughly between 9.30 am and 5 pm, with two late closings each week. There are several different reading rooms and enquiry areas including the Research Enquiries Room – where you can use the computer catalogues, order documents or discuss your research with the staff. Various indexes to the records and reference books can also be found there; the Document Reading Room – where you will read the more modern original documents; and the Map and Large Document Reading Room; the Microfilm Reading Room – where you can use the increasing number of records that can only be seen on microfilm. You do not need to order these documents, as the material is available in cabinets for you to help yourself. Records to be found there include surviving First World War service records for other ranks and a set of the 1901 Census on microfiche. Also worth knowing about is the Library, which is found off the Microfilm Reading Room, as it has a wide range of useful books and journals, including the *Gentleman's Magazine* and many trade and professional directories.

There is an extensive website at **www.pro.gov.uk**, which contains masses of information useful to family historians,

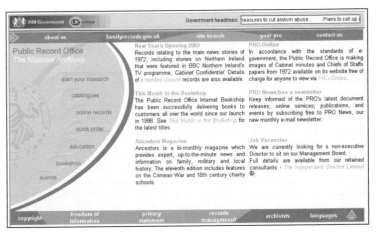

The Public Record Office (National Archives) website is another useful source of information online.

including many very useful leaflets explaining how to use the records. It also gives access to the NA's online catalogue PROCAT. The National Archives' records are arranged by the department which created the record. Each department is given a prefix (or lettercode), such as WO for War Office, FO for Foreign Office. Within each lettercode, the records are generally divided by type and put into series, which have a unique numerical number. Thus series WO 95 contains war diaries from the First World War; WO 96 contains militia service records before 1913; and WO 97 contains soldiers' documents before 1914. Within each series, individual items (known as *pieces*) have their own references, and it is these that you order. Descriptions of each piece number, together with broader descriptions of the series, are in PROCAT. At Kew you will find copies of what are known as the *series* or *class lists,* which are in effect paper copies of the electronic catalogue. On occasion you may find it easier to use these lists rather than the computer.

In addition to the National Archives, there is the National Library of Wales in Aberystwyth, the General Register Office and the National Archives of Scotland in Edinburgh, the Public Record Office of Northern Ireland (PRONI) in Belfast, and for Eire the National Archives of Ireland in Dublin. Each of these has a website with details of their holdings – addresses are given on pages 185–187.

Family Records Centre

The National Archives, together with the Office for National Statistics, runs the Family Records Centre (FRC) in central London. This is one of the major centres for family history in Britain and you will almost certainly need to use it in the course of your research. The Centre is open Monday to Saturday, roughly between 9.30 am and 5 pm, with two late closings. There is no charge and no need to make an appointment. In the basement are lockers, drinks machines and a place for you to eat your sandwiches. There is also a bookshop.

On the ground floor are the indexes to birth, marriage and death records from July 1837. You can also find details of some British subjects who were born, married or died abroad, the deaths and marriages of servicemen and adoptions since 1927. On the first floor is a complete set of census records for England and Wales, the Isle of

Man and the Channel Islands between 1841 and 1901, non-conformist church registers to 1837, and wills proved in the Prerogative Court of Canterbury before 1858. There are also extensive resources on CD-Rom and online. Helpful and knowledgeable staff are on hand who can point you in the right direction.

Local record offices and libraries

The next level is the county each with its own county record office (sometimes called an archive), occasionally with branches in different towns. In these are to be found records of local administration and justice: taxation and militia records, those of local businesses, deeds and other property records, poll books and electoral registers, education files and registers, and much else besides. Most of these archives also act as the local diocesan record office and house many ecclesiastical records, particularly parish registers and probate records before 1858.

It can sometimes be difficult to work out which record office has the documents you are looking for. However, help is at hand on the internet. Some eight million entries taken from catalogues at over 200 English archives are now available online as part of the Access to Archives initiative at **www.a2a.pro.gov.uk**. It is by no means complete; even so this is an amazing resource, particularly as it is extremely easy to use. Searches can be made by keyword or phrase, name, place, subject or date. The search results include the archive and its contact details, together with the archival reference. What you won't find, however, are many references to individuals, but only to the companies for which they worked, the churches they worshipped in and the colleges they attended. Another website offering similar information is the National Register of Archives (**www.hmc.gov.uk/nra**), although here you can't see the catalogue entries themselves.

Local studies libraries, which are less formally arranged and have many different names such as local history centres or local archives departments, are often housed in the county or borough central library. They can be a rich source for local specialist knowledge from the staff. They often have collections of local material such as plans, deeds, drawings and photographs that may not be available elsewhere, as well as local newspapers, electoral registers and books of local interest.

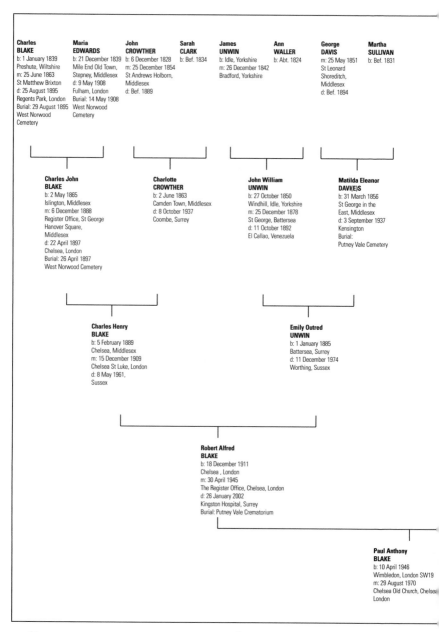

You can use computer programs to generate a family tree, such as this one showing the ancestry of Paul Blake.

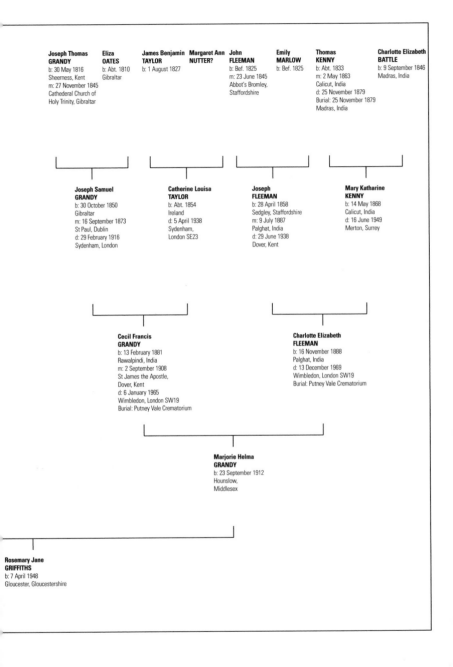

Joseph Thomas GRANDY
b: 30 May 1816
Sheerness, Kent
m: 27 November 1845
Cathederal Church of
Holy Trinity, Gibraltar

Eliza OATES
b: Abt. 1810
Gibraltar

James Benjamin TAYLOR
b: 1 August 1827

Margaret Ann NUTTER?

John FLEEMAN
b: Bef. 1825
m: 23 June 1845
Abbot's Bromley,
Staffordshire

Emily MARLOW
b: Bef. 1825

Thomas KENNY
b: Abt. 1833
m: 2 May 1863
Calicut, India
d: 25 November 1879
Burial: 25 November 1879
Madras, India

Charlotte Elizabeth BATTLE
b: 9 September 1846
Madras, India

Joseph Samuel GRANDY
b: 30 October 1850
Gibraltar
m: 16 September 1873
St Paul, Dublin
d: 29 February 1916
Sydenham, London

Catherine Louisa TAYLOR
b: Abt. 1854
Ireland
d: 5 April 1938
Sydenham,
London SE23

Joseph FLEEMAN
b: 28 April 1858
Sedgley, Staffordshire
m: 9 July 1887
Palghat, India
d: 29 June 1938
Dover, Kent

Mary Katharine KENNY
b: 14 May 1868
Calicut, India
d: 16 June 1949
Merton, Surrey

Cecil Francis GRANDY
b: 13 February 1881
Rawalpindi, India
m: 2 September 1908
St James the Apostle,
Dover, Kent
d: 6 January 1965
Wimbledon, London SW19
Burial: Putney Vale Crematorium

Charlotte Elizabeth FLEEMAN
b: 16 November 1888
Palghat, India
d: 13 December 1969
Wimbledon, London SW19
Burial: Putney Vale Crematorium

Marjorie Helma GRANDY
b: 23 September 1912
Hounslow,
Middlesex

Rosemary Jane GRIFFITHS
b: 7 April 1948
Gloucester, Gloucestershire

Recording information

If you speak to any 'old hand' they will probably admit that when they started their family history they didn't keep their notes in nearly as organised a way as they should have. Many of the more honest ones may admit that they still don't. Often the beginner is overtaken by enthusiasm and ignores the importance of keeping well-organised notes and files. You may believe that you can write it all up and file the papers properly later on – but you probably won't. So try not to get caught out by this trap: you will regret it in the long run. Start as you mean to go on and organise your records properly from the outset.

There are several ways of recording the information that you discover about your ancestors. There isn't a recommended system, as everybody has different needs. In the end it is down to personal choice. But whichever you choose, try to be consistent and don't skimp on paper or computer-readable media. Both loose-leaf binders and bound notebooks have their supporters. Separate sheets of paper kept in ring binders or lever-arch files enable you to move sheets from one file to another or to completely reorganise the papers as and when necessary. However, the danger of loss is greater than the notebook method, although this is less adaptable and you may also need a separate index so you can locate the information at a later date. Be warned, your collection will grow and the couple of ring binders you start out with may eventually become a dozen or more lever-arch files; the single notebook a whole shelf full. Whichever your choice, keep separate information on separate sheets, whether these are details about an individual person or a place.

In addition to your notes, you will also begin to accumulate copies of certificates, photocopies of documents and photographs of where your ancestors lived or worked, married or died. These are in addition to those that you will hopefully have received from relatives or already had in your own possession. Again these have to be well catalogued and filed.

An alternative is to record this information on computer. There are a number of programs that will enable you to do this. You can print out pedigree charts, family group sheets, ancestor charts and so on. You can add extra notes, stories and pictures for each individual. The advantage is that it enables you to manipulate

Even minor details can be useful in dating photographs, such as the style of these bicycles.

information quickly and easily to produce family trees and links between individuals and families. There are a number of programs available, which should cost no more than about £40 each. A number come with a dozen or so compact discs of data. In the shop this may seem like a great bargain, but on closer inspection they are almost always for American sources and are rarely of value to non-American researchers. Occasionally you may see a program given away free on the front cover of a computer magazine. The genealogical magazines have regular reviews and comparisons of these programs. Some programs also allow you to create websites and store digital images as well. However, there are dangers. Make sure that you back up your files at regular intervals, and print out hard copies on good-quality paper. To be on the safe side, you should keep copies of both computer disks and paper printouts in a separate location, just in case of a fire or other disaster – no amount of insurance can replace lost data! If you have backup files on disk, you should check them from time to time to make sure that they are still in good order.

Taking notes

Again it's easy to fall into bad habits when taking notes. It may seem obvious, but write clearly and copy exactly what is written in the document before you: don't abbreviate anything or expand it either. If it's a long, repetitious document, such as a will, then you may want to extract the essential information rather than make a full transcript. It goes without saying that you should try to be as legible as possible – there's nothing worse then getting home to find you can't read what you hastily scribbled down. An alternative might be to use a laptop computer or a PDA (such as a Psion Organiser or Palm Pilot) where you type the information directly into the machine.

You should always note down what you were looking for – particularly important if you don't find anything. If you find nothing, don't tear up the page but write down 'no entries found' or something similar: then you won't redo the search several years later having forgotten you have already done it.

An alternative is to obtain photocopies. Most libraries and record offices will allow copies to be made of the documents they hold, unless they are in very poor condition. The rules and charges vary considerably from one place to another but, if it is possible, then a photocopy has considerable advantages. It will be free from the copying mistakes you could have made; you can examine it more carefully and at length at home; and you will have, for posterity, a copy of the record that you so carefully sought and that probably mentions your ancestor by name. The only downside is that photocopies may be expensive and may take

As well as names and locations, details such as a club or school tie could give you more leads to follow up.

several weeks to be sent to you. A few record offices and libraries permit you to use your own camera to photograph their records, again with certain limitations, as this can be less damaging to the document than photocopying. Here the digital camera comes in to its own as you can actually see what you have taken before you leave for home. If you would like to use such a camera, you should ask the archivist on duty for permission.

Indexes

Much family history research involves using indexes of one sort or another. Very helpful they are too, although there are pitfalls for the unwary. The commonest misconception is that something that calls itself an index is somehow complete, but this is often not the case. Boyd's Marriage Index at the Society of Genealogists, for example, contains details of six million marriages between 1538 and 1837, but whole counties have never been indexed. Other indexes can more accurately be described as cumulative; that is they consist of information gathered from a variety of sources, and added to at intervals. The best-known example of this is the International Genealogical Index (IGI), which contains births, baptisms and marriages from the sixteenth century and even earlier. Several versions of this have been published over the years, first on microfiche, then on CD-Rom and the internet, each containing more entries than the previous one. This has now been supplemented by the British Isles Vital Records Index, which has a slightly higher proportion of recent records. Despite the millions of entries, there are still millions of ancestors who need to be found the old-fashioned way! A popular internet site is **www.freebmd.rootsweb.com**, an index to the General Register Office births, marriages and deaths; although incomplete, it can be useful nonetheless.

Another question you need to ask when using any index is 'how is it arranged?'. This is not the silly question it appears to be, since alphabetical order may not be the only element considered important by the indexer. Some indexes group together the spelling variants of particular surnames, which can be helpful, but only if the compiler's judgement on what is a variant of a particular name agrees with yours. Others may have only worked on the initial letter, ignoring the sequence that follows it. Look out for the way each index deals with particular kinds of names, like those starting with 'Mac' or Mc', for example. Double-barrelled surnames, names with prefixes like 'de' or 'van' etc. can also be dealt with in a number of ways, according to the decision of the compiler. Indexes are always helpful, but you should always be aware of what they are setting out to do and what their limitations are. Remember, when all else fails, read the instructions or ask the staff, who tend to be very aware of any shortcomings!

Sources

The records used in your family history research are many and varied, and were created for a variety of purposes, but genealogy was not usually one of them. These purposes might include the collection of taxes, recording a soldier's service, or the marking of religious rites of passage. It is therefore easy to become frustrated when the record you are looking at does not include the piece of information that would make it all so much easier. Look on the bright side: it gives you the opportunity to use all your skill and ingenuity to get at the evidence you need. After all, if you were not an incurable optimist, and tenacious with it, you would not have taken up family tree research in the first place!

Whatever source you are using, you should always try to think about the circumstances in which it was created, and how this might have affected its accuracy. It is remarkable how many people gave inaccurate information on their marriage certificates, either because they deliberately lied abut their age, for whatever reason, or unintentionally, simply because they were overcome with nerves!

Different documents contain different pieces of information, and by using several of them you may find that they complement each other, and the information in one source will enable you to locate another. For example, an army service record may enable you to locate the soldier's birth certificate, or a person's will might provide enough details to enable you to look for the births of his or her children.

If your family name is a very common one, you will probably find it much more helpful to use local records, particularly if your family has always lived in the same area. If you know that your family was associated with a particular church or school, it may be easier to search parish or school records than to try to find the birth

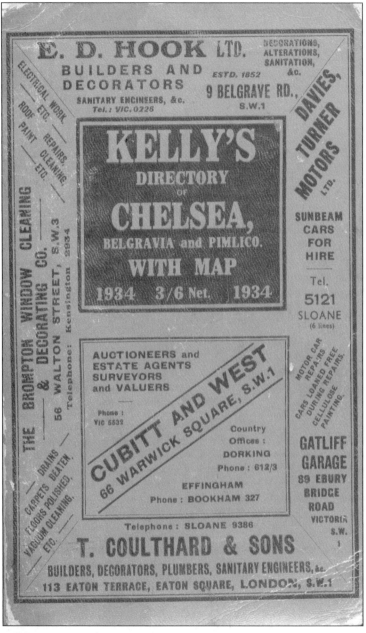

Kelly's Directory *of Chelsea for 1934.*

certificate for the right John Smith in the civil registration indexes. Conversely, if the name is a rare one, it is a good idea to note every instance of the surname that you find, and perhaps even attempt a systematic listing of every birth, marriage and death entry, etc. This is what members of the Guild of One-name Studies do, and such listings provide a valuable resource for anyone researching that name.

The internet

Computers and the internet have completely changed family history. The internet is now an essential part of research. Genealogy is one of the biggest success stories of the internet – it is the second or third most popular subject on the web. There are now tens of thousands of websites on family history, from government resources to personal sites devoted to a particular family. By its very nature the World Wide Web is a constantly changing animal. New sites arrive daily, almost hourly, any one of which may be useful, possibly essential, in your research. Sites also disappear or change their addresses (URLs in the jargon).

The internet is about global communication and the sharing of information. The availability and popularity of the web has made family history far simpler and more pleasurable and, coupled with traditional research methods, discovering your roots has never been easier or more rewarding. Indeed, if you do not use what is available online, then frankly you are hindering your research into your roots.

Even so, much, if not most, of your research will still have to involve old-fashioned legwork, visiting record offices and libraries, although an increasing amount of original documents are becoming available online. The 1901 Census is a prime example of this. If the web itself does not contain the answers, it can be an enormous help for beginners who are looking for information about where to start or for answers to more complex questions.

Most modern home computers come with a modem installed. All you have to do is to plug it into the phone line and register with a service provider and then you're ready to go. If you don't have a computer at home, you can gain access to the internet at large libraries, as they all have computers which can be used either for free or a nominal amount. In addition, there are usually staff available to help you get started and they may provide training courses as well. You may think that you're too old to master this new technology, but it is remarkably simple. And besides, when you're online, you can be as young as you like!

The biggest problem with the internet is finding exactly what you are after. Search engines will turn up various sites for you to visit. Perhaps the most comprehensive is Google at **www.google.co.uk** but there are a number of others as well. They all offer advice about how to refine your search, so that you don't end up trawling through hundreds of sites relating to Canadian real estate or American high schools.

Starting out

The BBC's history pages at **www.bbc.co.uk/history/your history** include a basic, but very helpful introduction to family history, including some useful links to other sites. One website that is useful as an introduction to records, archives and research in the United Kingdom, is maintained by the Historical Manuscripts Commission at **www.hmc.gov.uk/focus**.

Gateway sites

Gateway sites offer links to lots of other websites. The most important such genealogical site is Cyndi's List at **www.cyndislist.com**, conceived and run by Cyndi and Mark

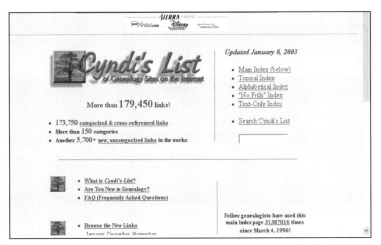

Cyndi's List website is a gateway site to a host of useful information online.

Howells in America. This has around 200,000 links to an array of sites covering every conceivable topic around the world. It is an absolute goldmine for anyone conducting any sort of genealogical research online, although it can sometimes be difficult to find exactly what you want. There is a specific page offering links to British websites at **www.cyndislist.com/uksites.htm**. The 'Are you new to genealogy?' link is an excellent beginner's guide and includes tips and links on how to research using specific resources, such as British birth, marriage and death records.

Another important American site which has considerable British material is **www.rootsweb.com**, with message boards, communities and databases to help you in the search for your ancestors. Of particular interest are the FreeBMD, FreeCEN and FreeREG projects which aim to put indexes to civil registration, censuses and parish registers online for free.

In Britain possibly the most valuable site is GenUKI (Genealogy UK and Ireland) at **www.genuki.org.uk**, a self-styled 'virtual reference library' operating as a clearing-house for family history research. Despite its rather bland appearance, its content is comprehensive and impressive. It includes a beginner's guide and lists of FAQs (frequently asked questions). The databases linked by GenUKI are arranged by county. Information here can be as diverse as examples of old handwriting and names of people executed for witchcraft. The GenUKI site includes reference to surname lists and

GenUKI website.

Ancestry.co.uk website.

mailing lists. Also worth looking at is **www.britishislesgenweb.org**, the British Isles GenWeb.

An increasing number of sites are charging for access to databases and other resources. The two biggest general genealogy sites are American based and therefore have a strong US bias: **www.genealogy.com** is purely American; **www.ancestry.co.uk** has considerable British content, including indexes and images for the 1891 and earlier censuses. These are subscription services for which you pay a fixed amount (£69.95 per year in 2003 for the Ancestry site). Other sites charge just for downloading the information you need. The National Archives chose this model for the 1901 Census (**www.census.pro.gov.uk**), where each page of the census costs 75p; the index itself is free. A similar site, which offers access to important indexes at the Society of Genealogists, is **www.englishorigins.com**. There is a fee (£6 in 2003) that allows you access to 150 entries but within a 48-hour period. The Federation of Family History Societies has its own pay-per-view site at **www.familyhistoryonline.net**, which offers access to indexes compiled by member societies.

Message boards and newsgroups

Talking to other people interested in family research can uncover new information and answer puzzling questions. This is where the internet really can come into its own as communication is easy, quick and cheap. There are two ways in which you can take advantage of this: message boards and newsgroups. Both are controlled to varying degrees by a webmaster or moderator who ensures that messages posted are relevant and that the personal details of members are kept secret.

Message boards are a superb way of asking specific questions and getting answers. It is important, however, to ensure that you post your messages to the correct board with the correct subject header. Rootsweb, already mentioned on page 69, hosts one of the most comprehensive message boards. Genforum, at **www.genforum.com**, boasts thousands of members and discussion groups dedicated to surnames, countries and counties. Many family history societies also have their own mailing lists and discussion groups. Ancestry.com also provides very helpful message boards.

There are also several newsgroups that the family historian will find useful. A complete list can be found at **www.genuki.org.uk/wg**. Some newsgroups are much more useful than others. It may be worth joining news.soc.genealogy.britain, news.soc.genealogy.ireland, news.soc.genealogy.methods and news.soc.genealogy.misc, which can offer intelligent discussion on genealogical matters, something which is lacking on many newsgroups.

CHAPTER 4

Basic Sources

This chapter shows you the principal sources for information to develop and extend your family tree.

Births, marriages and deaths from 1837

Birth, marriage and death certificates are undoubtedly the records you'll use most during the course of your researches. They are reasonably easy to track down, using indexes and then ordering copies of the certificates from the General Register Office.

The master set of indexes is at the Family Records Centre (FRC) in London. Copies (on microfiche or microfilm) can be found at many libraries (including the Society of Genealogists to 1920), local record offices and the National Archives. You can also check them online at **www.1837online.com** (for a fee) or at **http://freebmd.rootsweb.com/** to 1901 for free, although these latter indexes are far from complete and do not include entries that are less than 100 years old.

There is one series of index books for the whole of England and Wales. Up to 1983 they are arranged in quarters: January–March, April–June, July–September and October–December. From 1984, the volumes are annual. The country is divided into Registration Districts, each with a Superintendent Registrar in charge, and further divided into Sub-districts, under Registrars of Births and Deaths. The boundaries and names of these districts have changed over the years, and you can find details of this in *Registration Districts* by Ray Wiggins or Brett Langston's *A Handbook to the Civil Registration Districts of England and Wales.*

Births and deaths were recorded in special register books by local registrars. Every three months they were required to make copies of all the events registered, on the special forms provided, and send them to the Registrar General in London. It is from these copies that the General Register Office (GRO) in Southport issues copy certificates.

Application Number G003967

QDX 103586

CERTIFIED COPY   **OF AN ENTRY**

	DEATH	Entry No.	289

Registration district **BLACKPOOL AND FYLDE**   Administrative area

Sub-district **BLACKPOOL**   County of Lancashire

1. Date and place of death *Thirteenth August 1975*
Victoria Hospital. Blackpool

2. Name and surname *John BERRY*

3. Sex *Male*

4. Maiden surname of woman who has married —

5. Date and place of birth *1 March 1898*
Ancoats. Greater Manchester

6. Occupation and usual address *Sorting clerk (retired)*
49 Kylemore Avenue. Blackpool

7. (a) Name and surname of informant *(16)*
Mary Elizabeth Brown

(b) Qualification *Sister*

(c) Usual address *13 Holborne Avenue. Toronto M4c 2P5 Canada*

8. Cause of death
1a Bronchopneumonia
1. Diabetes.

Certified by Lewlees m.b.

9. I certify that the particulars given by me above are true to the best of my knowledge and belief *Mary E. Brown*   Signature of informant

10. Date of registration *Thirteenth August 1975*

11. Signature of registrar *W.T. McKend Registrar*

Sixteen W.T. McK

CERTIFIED to be a true copy of an entry in the certified copy of a register of Deaths in the District above mentioned. Given at the GENERAL REGISTER OFFICE, under the Seal of the said Office on *15th January 1992*

This certificate is issued in pursuance of the Births and Deaths Registration Act 1953. Section 34 provides that any certified copy of an entry purporting to be sealed or stamped with the seal of the General Register Office shall be received as evidence of the birth or death to which it relates without any further or other proof of the entry, and no certified copy purporting to have been given in the said Office shall be of any force or effect unless it is sealed or stamped as aforesaid.

A death certificate from 1969 or later contains information about the person's date and place of birth, which can usually take you directly to their birth certificate. In this case, the informant was John Berry's sister, who gave his correct date of birth but the wrong year!

For marriages the situation is a little different, as they are not arranged in sub-districts, but according to the place of marriage. Most registrars of marriages may also be registrars of births and deaths. In addition, Church of England clergy are entitled to perform marriages. Since 1898 other people, known as Authorised Persons (generally nonconformist and Catholic clergy), have been able to apply for a licence to perform marriages. These registrars also submit quarterly returns of their marriages to the Registrar General via their local Superintendent Registrar.

The indexes, whether for births, deaths or marriages, are arranged alphabetically by surname, then forename, and give the district where the event was registered, then a volume and a page number, which identifies the page in the quarterly returns where the full entry can be found. From the September quarter of 1911, birth indexes include the maiden surname of the child's mother, and, from the March quarter of 1912, marriage indexes show the surname of the other party to the marriage. Death indexes include the age at death from 1866, and the actual date of birth since 1969.

When searching for a birth, you should not only look in the year when you expect the birth to have taken place, but also a year, or even two, either side. Six weeks are allowed for registering a birth, so even when you have an exact date of birth, the entry may appear in the quarter after the one you expect. Ages given on marriage certificates or from family information are not always reliable, so it is wise to keep an open mind, and try to check with more than one source if possible.

You need to note down from the index the registration district and volume and page number before you can order a certificate, either in person at the FRC or by post from the General Register Office in Southport. Special forms are provided for both kinds of order, but if you send an order by post direct to Southport you can simply write or type your request clearly, if you prefer. Forms for postal application can also be downloaded from their website **www.statistics.gov.uk**. Eventually you will be able to order certificates directly via their website. You can also order certificates by phone if you have the full details. Certificates ordered in person cost £7 (in 2003). You can either collect them from the FRC after four working days or have them posted to you, which takes a day longer. Orders by post cost £8.50 (in 2003) provided you have the full reference. If you cannot find a copy of

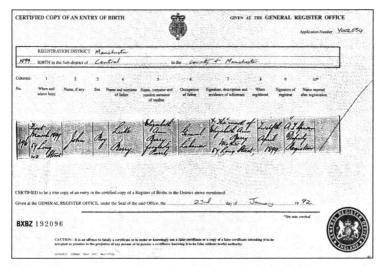

Birth certificates are among the most useful documents for family history research.

the indexes, GRO at Southport will carry out limited searches for you, for an extra fee. Alternatively you can hire a researcher to locate and order certificates for you. Some family history societies also provide a search service for their members.

When you place your order at the FRC, you will have the choice of a full or a short birth certificate. You should order a full certificate, as a short certificate shows only the name and date of birth and is of no use for family history.

In theory, you can work back through the civil registration records, alternating between birth and marriage certificates, each of which gives the information you need for the next search.

As well as the registration district and sub-district, you will find the following details on a birth certificate:

- Name (if any) and sex of the child
- Date and place of birth (if the time is given, this may indicate a multiple birth)
- Name and surname of the father
- Name, surname and maiden name of the mother
- Father's occupation
- Name and address of the informant (almost always one of the parents)
- Date of registration

Armed with the names of both parents you can then search back through the indexes for their marriage. When searching for a marriage, you are looking for a matching pair of entries for the bride and groom, in the same quarter, with the same volume and page number. A marriage certificate shows the following, in addition to the name of the registration district:

- Date and place of the marriage
- According to which religious rites, if any
- Whether by banns, licence or Registrar's certificate
- Names, ages, occupations and addresses of both parties
- Names and occupations of the fathers of both parties
- Signatures of two or more witnesses

The ages tell you where to look for their births, and the names of the fathers can be used to check if you have the right birth entry, about which more detail is given below.

English and Welsh death certificates before 1969 are less informative than those of many other countries. Their main weakness is that they do not give the date or place of birth of the deceased person, so that the information they contain does not lead easily to another stage of research in the way that birth and marriage certificates do. They may still provide valuable information, such as the name and address of the informant, who may be a close relative. From the June quarter of 1969, the situation improves greatly, as the date and place of birth are given, and if the deceased is a woman who is or has been married, her maiden name is shown. It is should now be a straightforward matter to find the person's birth entry. The date of birth is also shown in the death indexes from June 1969, and this alone will usually be enough for you to locate the birth, but if the name is a common one and there is more than one possible birth entry for them, you will need to buy the death certificate itself to find out the place of birth.

Death certificates before June 1969 show the registration district and sub-district, and give the following information:

- Date and place of death
- Full name and age of the deceased
- Cause of death
- Name, address, and qualification of the informant
- Date of registration

If the deceased is a woman, her marital status will be indicated; if she is unmarried, her father's name might also be given. If the death is of a child, the father's name will sometimes be given.

If you have little idea of when an ancestor died, you may have a long search, for little apparent gain. One way of narrowing the search may be to look for an ancestor's will, which is usually a much quicker process. Despite some of the problems, death certificates are certainly of interest, and you should always try to 'kill off' your ancestors. Details of relationships within the family are likely to be of most interest; for example if a woman is shown as a wife or a widow, this tells you whether to look before or after that date for her husband's death. If the death was in a hospital or workhouse, there may be records that could shed light on the individual's last days. You should also note the cause of death, even if you do not understand it! If you do not happen to have a medical dictionary, there is a useful website that explains many of the causes of death, which you will find at **http://cancerweb. ncl.ac.uk/omd**.

In addition, if your ancestor died a sudden or untimely death, there should have been an inquest, the date and place of which is noted on the death certificate. You may be able to follow this up in Coroners' records, but in practice it is often much easier to look for reports in the local newspaper.

If you are researching a common surname, you may well find several possible entries for a birth, so you will need to find some way of identifying the right one. If you know that a particular piece of information of which you are certain will appear on the certificate, you can ask to have the entry checked to see if it agrees. The certificate will only be issued if it matches the piece of information you have given, known as a 'checking point'. If it does not, you will instead be given a refund of part of the fee (£4 in 2003). Space is provided for this on the back of the forms in the FRC, with suggested checking points, the most usual of which is the father's name on a birth certificate. Even using this procedure it can prove expensive to have several entries checked, so it is a good idea to narrow the range of possibilities first, using information from other sources, such as census returns. Another tip is to eliminate one or more of the birth entries by finding corresponding death entries which show that the child died soon after birth and could not have grown up to become your ancestor. This only works when the

BOU—BOW   BIRTHS registered in July, August, and Septe[mber]

Name	District	Vol	Page
BOULDEN, Jane.	Helston	5c.	219
—— Josiah.	Helston	5c.	212
BOULDIN, Catherine.	Lambeth	1d.	236
BOULDING, Florence.	Sheffield	9c.	328
BOULDRY, Emily Jane.	Truro	5a.	166
BOULDS, Charles Edward.	Woolwich	1d.	663
—— William.	Plymouth	5b.	294
BOULORE, Abraham Joseph.	Colchester	4a.	277
BOULOIER, Sarah Ann.	Leeds	9b.	397
BOULLEN, Emily Frances.	Manchester	8d.	236
—— Sarah Ann.	Liverpool	8b.	149
BOULERER, Edward George.	Shaftesbury	5a.	235
BOULETRIDGE, Charlotte.	Atherstone	6d.	372
BOULT, Amelia Sarah.	Pancras	1b.	45
—— Ellen.	Sunderland	10a.	471
—— Frederick Arthur.	Wolstanton	6b.	99
BOULTBER, Hugh Edmund.	Leeds	9b.	465
—— Mary Ann.	Chesterfield	7b.	500
BOULTBY, George.	Nottingham	7b.	233
BOULTER, Adelaide Eliza.	Woodbridge	4a.	615
—— Alfred.	Presteigne	11b.	147
—— Alfred George.	Halstead	4a.	347
—— Charles.	Poplar	1c.	614
—— Clarissa Martha.	Bristol	6a.	31
—— Edgar John.	Woodbridge	4a.	615
—— Eliza Maria.	Blaby	7a.	35
—— Elizabeth.	Leicester	7a.	228
—— John.	Cricklade	5a.	26
—— Julia Brett.	Mitford	4b.	357
—— Lucy Jane.	Leicester	7a.	188
—— Mary Holdich.	Blaby	7a.	33
—— Rosina Jane.	Shoreditch	1c.	111
—— Sarah.	Upton	6c.	313
—— Sarah Jane.	Westbury, W.	5a.	136
—— Walter George.	Loddon	4b.	206
—— William Albert.	Bristol	6a.	49
BOULTING, Alice Maria E.	Marylebone	1a.	414
BOULTON, Agnes Emma.	Bristol	6a.	28
—— Albert.	Cricklade	5a.	30
—— Albert Edward.	Shoreditch	1c.	91
—— Albert James.	Cirencester	6a.	330
—— Anne Elizabeth.	Louth	7a.	506
—— Annie Louisa.	Westminster, St. M.	1a.	376
—— Annie Maria.	Beverley	9d.	91
—— Annie Maria.	Edmonton	3a.	171
—— Arthur Joseph.	Shoreditch	1c.	91
—— Benjamin.	Shifnal	6a.	591
—— Elizabeth Ann.	Barton	6a.	541
—— Ellen.	Clifton	6a.	101
—— Emily.	Stafford	6b.	2
—— Emily.	Glanford B.	7a.	654
—— Emma.	Evesham	6c.	322
—— Ephraim.	Stoke T.	6b.	171
—— Ernest Vivian.	Hackney	1b.	413
—— Flora.	Chipping S.	6a.	161
—— Frances.	Newcastle L.	6b.	73
—— Fred.	Rotherham	9c.	646
—— Frederic James.	Stourbridge	6c.	210
—— Frederick Harry.	Portsea	2b.	426
BOURNE, Joseph Guy.	I. Wight	2b.	837
—— Kate.	Islington	1b.	282
—— Margaret Barnside M.	Tynemouth	10b.	164
—— Marian.	Blean	2a.	688
—— Mary.	Stoke T.	6b.	249
—— Mary Eleanor.	Newmarket	3b.	652
—— Mary Ellen.	Dudley	6a.	46
—— Sarah Jane.	W. Derby	8b.	336
—— Sarah Jane.	St. Alban's	3a.	343
—— Sarah Louisa.	Canterbury	2a.	674
—— Thomas.	Droitwich	6a.	361
—— Walter Fox.	Hampstead	1a.	565
—— Walter James.	Ashborne	7b.	477
—— William.	Hartley	5c.	264
—— William Ernest.	Ashby Z.	7a.	90
—— William Richard.	W. Ashford	2a.	635
—— Male.	Droitwich	6a.	361
—— Male.	Droitwich	6a.	361
BOURNER, Caroline Harriett.	Kingston	2a.	253
—— Charles Henry.	Trotterden	2a.	627
—— Charlotte Augusta.	Hailsham	2b.	63
—— Joseph.	Kingston	2a.	253
—— Louisa Mary.	Windsor	2c.	413
BOURTON, Ada.	Reading	2c.	359
—— James.	Hungerford	2c.	244
—— Mary Jane.	Hungerford	2c.	244
BOUSER, Jane.	Chesterfield	7b.	537
BOUSFIELD, Anthony.	Manchester	8d.	280
—— George William.	Hampstead	1a.	667
—— Mary Elizabeth.	Kendal	10b.	644
—— Sarah.	E. Ward	10b.	607
BOUSKILL, Elizabeth Isabella.	Preston	8e.	583
—— Julia Ann.	Lancaster	8e.	683
BOUSTEAD, Annie Elizabeth.	Wigton	10b.	482
—— Susannah.	Carlisle	10b.	472
BOUSTRED, Pauline.	Edmonton	3a.	170
BOUTELL, Elizabeth Alice.	Tendring	4a.	270
BOUTFLOUR, Charles F.	Westminster, St. J.	1a.	349
BOUTLE, Alice Louisa.	Ware	3a.	209
BOUTWOOD, Charles John.	Hastings	2b.	20
BOUVERIE, Jacob.	Faringdon	2c.	249
BOVEA, Harriet Ann.	Leeds	9b.	493
BOVETT, Edwin James.	Honiton	5b.	32
BOVEY, Blanch Tucker.	Totnes	5b.	177
BOVIL, Philip.	Cambridge	3b.	499
BOVILL, Elizabeth.	S. Shields	10a.	610
—— Hugh George.	Epsom	2a.	25
BOVILLE, Charles Henry.	Northallerton	9d.	493
BOVINGDON, George Henry.	Berkhampstead	3a.	402
—— Sarah Jane.	Islington	1b.	227
BOVINGTON, Susan Elizabeth.	Eton	3a.	435
BOVIS, Ernest Edward W.	Medway	2a.	413
BOW, Mary Ann.	Merthyr T.	11a.	397
—— Samuel.	Bristol	6a.	14
BOWATER, Florence Mary.	Birmingham	6d.	19
—— Kate Amelia.	Sheffield	9c.	407
—— Richard Edwin.	Wolverhampton	6b.	476
BOWCHER, James.	Gt. Boughton	8a.	361
BOWCOCK, Frederick.	Manchester	8d.	165

An example of a page in a birth index volume in the style which was used from 1866 to 1910. Before this date, the indexes were handwritten; after that they were typed and then eventually produced by computer.

entries are in different registration districts and after 1866, when ages appear in the death indexes.

It is possible you won't find an entry at all in the indexes. There are a number of reasons for this. In the early years, many births, and some deaths, were not registered, partly through evasion or ignorance, and partly because the original legislation was badly drafted. This was remedied in 1874, so after that date if the entry you seek does not appear it is much more likely to be have been mis-indexed, or even omitted altogether from the national indexes. By the time you see an entry in the index, it has been copied at least three times, and errors could have crept in at each stage. It is always possible that the event took place abroad for some reason. A marriage may not be found because it never took place at all, or was after the birth of the child. Sometimes the mother will have been married before, so she did not marry under her maiden name.

Marriages might also have taken place outside England and Wales. If a couple married very young and you cannot find an entry, they may have eloped to Scotland. Scots law and registration systems are quite different from those of England and Wales and, before the age of majority was reduced to 18, under-age persons who wished to marry without their parents' consent might cross the border to Gretna Green, where they could marry at 16. Anywhere in Scotland would have done, but Gretna was popular because it was the first place on the Scottish side of the border. It might not have been the wisest choice, however, as it was the first place that the parents of runaways thought of looking. If you think that a couple may have eloped, you will need to consult the indexes of the General Register Office for Scotland. The Scotland's People website **www.scotlandspeople.gov.uk** will tell you more about this, or write to the GROS in Edinburgh.

The government is thinking about radically revising the whole system of civil registration, which will have serious implications for family history. If the current proposals are adopted, records relating to persons born more than a hundred years ago will be open to inspection, possibly online or at local record offices. There will be restrictions on what can be seen on the more recent certificates, such as an individual's occupation, address or cause of death. If changes are made, they are unlikely to be fully implemented before 2007 or 2008 at the earliest.

The 1901 and other censuses

One of the most useful and popular sources used in family history research is the census. It has also been one of the best known outside the immediate circle of family historians since the Public Record Office took the unprecedented step of putting the whole of the 1901 Census, fully indexed, on the internet. This ambitious enterprise attracted a great deal of press attention when it was first launched, not least because the demand was so overwhelming that the system could not cope, and the site was not fully operational until some months after its intended start date of January 2002. It is now working normally.

A census is particularly helpful to family historians because everyone should appear in it, usually with their family and neighbours, so that you get a picture of them in the context of their surroundings. The major drawback of the census as a source is that it contains personal information about individuals, so it is closed to public inspection for 100 years. This means that the most recent census we can look at is for 1901, so you have a whole century and more of your family's history to investigate before you come to this

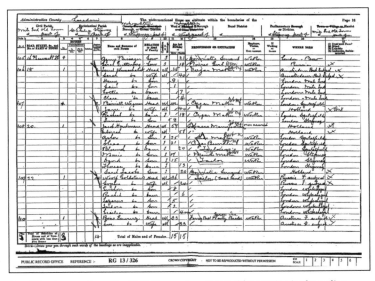

Providing images from the 1901 Census is a charged-for service in the online version of the 1901 Census, but if you know the address where your ancestor was on census night, you can search the microfilm or microfiche version.

wonderful resource. Dates of the 1841 and subsequent censuses are given in Appendix D on page 175.

The census has been taken in Britain every ten years since 1801, except for 1941, so most adults will have a memory of filling in the forms. The forms to which we have become accustomed are much longer and more detailed than those for the censuses we use in family history research. In the past, as now, forms (called schedules) were distributed to each household to be completed with the details of every person who was there on census night, whether or not they were normally resident there. There were special forms for institutions like hospitals, barracks and so on. In 1891 and 1901 the following details were recorded for each person:

- Name and surname
- Relationship to the head of the household
- Marital status
- Age and sex
- Occupation, and whether they were an employer, employee, working on their own account or working at home
- Birthplace
- Details of infirmities or disabilities
- *In Wales only,* whether the person spoke Welsh, English or both

From 1851 to 1881 the same information was recorded, except for the details about whether a person was an employer or an employee, and the language spoken. In 1841 the surname, forename and occupation were asked for, and whether or not they were born in the same county, or in Ireland, Scotland or abroad; ages over 15 were rounded down to the nearest five years.

When the schedules had been completed for each household, they were collected by the enumerator who had delivered them in the first place. He or she then copied the details from the schedules into an enumeration book. The enumeration books were bound together in sub-districts and districts, the same divisions used for civil registration of births, marriages and deaths. Registrars and Superintendent Registrars were responsible for collecting the books from the enumerators and sending them to the GRO in London.

The 1901 Census can be consulted in two different ways. The more popular method is the online version, which can be found at **www.census.pro.gov.uk**. This is searchable by name, so you do not need to know exactly where your ancestors were on census night to find them. There are basic and advanced search facilities, and a great deal of help can be found on the site for you to get the best out of your searches. If you do not find them at first, there are wild card searches – very useful if the name does not appear exactly as you expect it, either because the enumerator copied it incorrectly or the transcriber for the online project did so. Any genuine transcription errors can be reported through the website, and will be corrected after checking. The search result will show the person's name and age, their birthplace and occupation, and the place where they appear in the census, though not the exact address or full reference.

Once you have found a likely entry or entries for the person you want, you can click on a link to view either an image of the actual census page where they appear or a full transcript of the individual's entry. There is a charge for this, and you can pay either by credit card, debit card or by voucher. Vouchers can be bought from the National Archives at Kew, at the Family Records Centre, or you can order them through the website. You can also obtain them through many family history societies and some record offices and libraries. The minimum charge for either a voucher or credit card payment is £5 in 2003. Payment by voucher is the better method, since a voucher is valid for six months from the time when you start using it, but a credit card session lasts only 48 hours, so you lose any unused credit after this time. In 2003, the charge was 75p per image or 50p for a transcript. When you see the image, it is of the whole census page which can contain up to 30 people, including the other members of the household. You can print out the image or save it on your own computer, or order high-quality A3 prints through the website. You can also use this service on site at the Family Records Centre and at the National Archives at Kew, where you can make self-service laser copies. Many record offices and libraries also provide the online service.

The 1901 Census website may be your first experience of looking at the census, or even your first foray into family history research, but you will soon discover that most census searching is still done on microfilm or microfiche. The Family Records Centre has a complete set of census returns for 1841–1901 for England, Wales, the Channel Islands and the Isle of Man; and the National Archives at Kew has the 1901 Census only on microfiche. Most record offices and libraries also have microfiche or microfilm copies for their own geographical area.

Person Result List

If you find the text difficult to read because of its size, click here to find out how to enlarge it.

⌐⌐ = View the image of the original document (chargeable).

A Name= View this individual's details (chargeable)

▶ **Results:** 1-4 of 4 Matches

£						
Image	**Name**	**Age**	**Where Born**	**Administrative County**	**Civil Parish**	**Occupation**
	Edward Furminger	12	Kent Sittingbourne	Kent	Sittingbourne	
	Edward Furminger	14	Kent Lower Halstow	Of Kent	Sittingbourne	Stone Breaker
	Edward Furminger	35	Kent Maidstone	Of Kent	Sittingbourne	General Dealer Shop
	Edward Furminger	58	Kent Maidstone	Kent	Sittingbourne	General Laborer

Found it? you can...

- view the image of the original document by clicking on the image icon ⌐⌐ to the left of the person's name. **There is a charge for this.**
- view the full transcription details by clicking on the underlined name A Name. **There is a charge for this.**

  how much does it cost, how do I pay?

  [you will be asked to pay when you first select a chargeable service] - if you don't have a session

  🖨 Netscape users - for help on printing this page click here.

Not found it?

- too many results
- not found the right person
- click here to go back and search again

The 1901 Census person search result in the online version of the 1901 Census is free to use, but there is a charge if you want to view the transcription of an entry or the image of a census page.

When you search the census on microfilm or microfiche, you will need to learn how to search for a place or exact address, most of which do not yet have name indexes. There are clear instructions on how to do this at the FRC and there are staff on hand to help you. Every page in the census has a unique identifier, made up of several elements. All 1901 Census references begin with RG 13, followed by three other numbers: a piece number, a folio number and a page number. A piece is simply one of the many groups into which the many thousands of census enumerators' books are divided. They are of varying sizes, and each contains a number of enumerators' books. Within each piece, every other page is stamped with a folio number, so a piece number and a folio number will identify a pair of pages, the page with the folio number on it and the following page. Each individual page is also numbered, but the page numbering starts at 1 at the beginning of every enumeration book, and there are several books in each piece, so the page number is not unique, which is why the folio number is the important one. This makes a lot more sense when you are looking at an actual film or fiche, rather than reading about it in a book, so do not be put off.

There are a number of name indexes to parts of some census years, but so far 1881 is the only year, apart from 1901 where there is a complete index and transcription. This can be consulted on microfiche, on CD-Rom or through the FamilySearch website. For other years there are indexes to some areas, which vary in format as they were compiled by different people at different times. The FRC and Society of Genealogists both have good collections of these. Details of many of them can be found in *Marriage and Census Indexes* by Jeremy Gibson and Elizabeth Hampson.

Some digitised census images can be seen on the internet and on CD-Rom, and many more will follow, as the National Archives has granted licences to a number of commercial companies to provide these services. As yet there are very few indexes to accompany the images, but this will not always be the case.

There are some other problems with the census. Some returns may be damaged or even missing altogether – 1861 is a particularly bad year for this. The information given may not always be very accurate, as people sometimes did not know their exact age or birthplace. If they could not read and write, the enumerator may have misheard their answers, and if they could write they may have had illegible handwriting. Unfortunately, in every census some people are omitted, either accidentally or because they were deliberately avoiding it. Perhaps they were hiding because they thought the enumerator was the rent man! This is not much help if your ancestor is the one who resists all attempts to find them, but you are unlikely to be unlucky on all your lines. Remember that however detailed and useful a source may be, it is always possible that you will be able to get the information you need by some other means. It is the information that is important and not the source itself, which is just a means to that end.

When you have found at least some of your ancestors in the 1901 Census, you are nicely poised to take your researches back into the nineteenth century and beyond. Most of the sources you will have used for the twentieth century are also applicable to earlier periods, perhaps in a different form, and there are many others that you will encounter as your research progresses. The important thing is that you have learned how to use the sources you consult, and put your findings together to construct a family tree, which you will add to as you continue with your quest.

Parish records

When you start to trace your ancestors back into the early nineteenth century, you'll increasingly have to rely on parish registers. In some ways this is good because there are several comprehensive indexes. However, the records were often poorly kept or just do not survive, which can make using them very frustrating.

The Anglican Church, or Church of England, is the Established Church in England (and to 1920 in Wales). There were (and indeed still are) some 16,000 Anglican parishes across England and Wales – most villages were within a single parish, although towns had two or more parishes depending on their size and the wealth of benefactors in medieval times. If the clergy and their clerks were conscientious, then that is a great bonus for family historians. But often, of course, many baptisms, marriages and burials were either not recorded or incompletely noted in the register and are thus lost for good. Although it has not been a legal requirement for everyone to use the Established Church since 1689, from 1754 to 1837 it was the only place (apart from Quaker Meeting Houses and synagogues) where marriages could legally be performed in England and Wales.

Parish registers were first ordered to be kept in 1538, although few records survive before the beginning of the seventeenth century. The only major change since then was the introduction of printed forms in 1754 for marriages, and 1813 for baptisms and burials, into which specified details have to be entered. In the baptism registers are spaces for the name of the child, the forename and surname of the parents, the father's occupation and the abode of the family. The entry is only required to show the date of baptism, not date of birth, although this is sometimes added. The other significant disadvantage of baptism entries compared with birth certificates is that they do not include the mother's maiden name. Burial registers also follow the pattern established in 1813, and show only the name and abode of the deceased, their age, and the date of burial. This is much less information than appears on a death certificate, which includes the cause of death.

The survival of early registers is patchy, and they can be depressingly unhelpful. Baptismal entries are often little more than the child's name, who the father was, and when the event took place. Baptisms normally occurred within a few days of the birth. If the child was born out of wedlock, this would also be noted and the mother's name given. Before 1754, entries for weddings usually contain the names of the spouses, with perhaps a note if one of them was born outside the parish. After 1754, however, marriage entries had to be entered in special registers and are a little more informative.

If the register you are looking for is missing, it is worth seeing whether a duplicate, known as a bishop's transcript, survives. From 1598, parish clerks had to make regular copies and send them to the bishop for safekeeping. However, as this task was unpaid it was not always done and the quality of the transcript is often poor.

Most parish registers and bishop's transcripts are deposited at local record offices. It is now rare for individual churches to keep their old registers, although country parishes may have registers in current use that go back a century or more. *The Phillimore Atlas and Index of Parish Registers* will tell you where registers are held. Most archives and local libraries have copies.

A large number of registers have been transcribed and published. The largest collection of transcripts is with the Society of Genealogists. Details of what exactly they have can be found on their website or in a series of county booklets published by the Society.

Another important index at the SoG is Boyd's Marriage Index, which includes details of about one in eight marriages between 1538 and 1837. The Index is gradually being put online at **www.englishorigins.net**, where it can be searched for a fee, or you can consult it in book form for free in the Society's Library.

However, the most important index is the International Genealogical Index (IGI), which includes details of people mostly before about 1837 in parish registers. The Index, however, covers only births, christenings and marriages. It is by no means complete, and is not entirely accurate, but even so it is an extremely useful tool. It is available on microfiche, and as part of the FamilySearch program on CD-Rom and online at **www.familysearch.org**. The British Isles Vital Records Index supplements the IGI but is currently only available on CD-Rom. Both the IGI and VRI are produced by the Latter-day Saints church.

The Federation of Family History Societies publishes the National Burial Index (NBI), which complements the IGI by indexing burial registers. Coverage is patchy, but should improve greatly in future editions. This is only available on CD, although a few indexes are available online (for a small fee) at **www.familyhistoryonline.net**. Your local family history society should have a copy of the NBI and it should also be available at local reference libraries.

During the eighteenth century, more and more people were attracted by other Christian sects, especially Methodism which seemed both to be more vital and answer doctrinal questions in a more contemporary way than the Church of England. In general these nonconformists, as they were known, were tolerated, although only Anglicans could be officers in the forces or attend university and only Church of England register entries were admissible as evidence in law. The position was very different for Roman Catholics, who remained actively discriminated against until the end of the eighteenth century.

Many nonconformists continued to use the parish church for christenings, marriages and funerals. In addition, a number of people changed religious denominations at various times in their lives. A self-made businessman might start as a Methodist, but become a pillar of the Church of England once he made his fortune.

On the setting up of the new central system of births, marriages and deaths in 1837, the government asked nonconformist churches to send in their registers, and most complied. These registers are with the National Archives and copies can be seen at the Family Records Centre and in the Microfilm Reading Room at Kew. Most of the birth and baptism entries are included in the IGI or British Isles Records Index. A central registry, at Dr William's Library in London, also keeps details of births from 1742 to 1857 submitted by individuals. Again these records are at the NA and FRC.

Nonconformist registers after 1837 have either been deposited with local record offices or are still with individual churches or chapels. Some transcripts have been made and copies are often to be found at the Society of Genealogists.

Catholic churches were also asked to send in their registers, but relatively few did so. Because Catholicism was illegal until the 1780s and then only permitted with restrictions until 1830, relatively few records survive. Most parish registers are still kept by the church. There are records of fines, and other penalties, imposed upon Recusants (that is people who remained Catholics) in the National Archives and in Quarter Session records at local record offices. The SoG has transcripts of some parish records and other material about Catholics. The Catholic Central Library, Lancing Street, London NW1 1ND (020 7383 4333) also has considerable resources.

Family historians naturally tend to ignore parish registers after 1837 as the certificates are much more informative and easier to obtain. In fact, for a number of reasons, parish records can still be useful. The first is that when you know that a family was associated with a particular church for a number of years, a single register may well contain several family baptisms (and possibly weddings and burials) which you can quickly identify. You may only really be interested in your direct ancestor; however, the parish register provides a low-cost method of filling in details about the rest of the family. If the family has a very common surname, it may be easier to locate a baptism in the church register than to order several birth certificates until you find the right one.

The information on marriage certificates is the same as on church marriage registers which you can consult at little or no cost if the register is held at a local record office. There are other reasons for wanting to look at a church marriage register. You can look at original signatures, and the full details of the original entry that may not always have been accurately copied in the quarterly returns to the GRO. The context of the entry can also be very revealing. For example, other entries in the register may be for members of the same family, and you may even occasionally find a double wedding. Another benefit of looking at a range of entries is that you may find the clergyman or parish clerk was slapdash in his record-keeping. This is particularly significant if you have a marriage certificate where no father's name is given for one or both parties. The usual conclusion would be that the person concerned was illegitimate, but when you look at the register you just may find that it was badly kept, and no one married in that parish appears to have been born in wedlock!

The burial registers are less likely to be helpful, but they may still have their uses, particularly if the parish is a rural one. If there were a large number of deaths in a short period this may well indicate that the area was suffering from an epidemic or occasionally even famine. It can provide a quick way of locating deaths of various family members in one go, but from the middle of the nineteenth century increasing numbers of burials were not in churchyards but in cemeteries, so for many people the use of church burial registers is simply not an option. However, where there are churchyard burials in the early years of Civil Registration, they may contain burials of people whose deaths were not properly registered.

Another little-used source is the parish magazine, which normally includes brief details of baptisms, marriages and burials. The first magazines date from the beginning of the nineteenth century. Unfortunately relatively few survive, but where they do they are often found at local studies libraries.

Wills and probate

A national system of recording wills began in 1858. Annual indexes were produced from that date for the whole of England and Wales, which makes finding wills and probate relatively simple. If your ancestor left a will, it may contain all kinds of valuable information about them and their families, so it is well worth looking to find out if they did. Fortunately this is easy to do, and even the indexes themselves contain a wealth of detail. About 10 per cent of people left a will in 1900, but most individuals had so few possessions that they were amicably (or otherwise) divided between relations on their decease without any legal involvement.

Unlike most kinds of records you consult during your research, wills were written with the future in mind. Though not addressed directly to the family historian, a will is concerned with the family line and is likely to include specific information on relationships within the family.

Since they are legal documents, they also contain a good deal of legal jargon, which may be daunting at first, but mainly consists of a few key terms with which you will soon become familiar. The process by which a will is dealt with by the court is called *probate,* and when this process is complete, the will has been *proved.* The person who makes a will is the *testator,* and he or she appoints in the will one or more *executors,* who carry out their instructions. This means the distribution of their assets, also called their *estate.* Those in receipt of these bequests, or legacies, are called *beneficiaries* or *legatees.* To be valid, a will had to be signed by the testator and two witnesses. Witnesses could not be beneficiaries of the will, but executors could be, and often were.

If a person died without leaving a will, but there was property which needed to be dealt with, they were said to be intestate. The next of kin, or some other interested party, could apply for *letters of administration,* often abbreviated to 'admons', which allowed them to distribute the deceased's money and goods according to the law at the time. The details varied over the years, but generally speaking the estate would be divided between the surviving spouse and any legitimate children. Where there was no spouse or children, the person's parents or brothers and sisters would be the legal heirs. *Whitaker's Almanac* for the year in which the person died will include a section about the state of the law regarding intestacy at the time. People who applied for letters of administration were called *administrators,* and in some cases were appointed where there was a perfectly valid will, but the executors named in it were not able to perform their duties, possibly because they had died.

When there is a will there are two documents to look at: the will itself and the *grant of probate.* If the index indicates an administration, then there will only be a grant of administration. Grants of probate and administration are very similar, and are simply one-page documents, usually giving little or no more information than is in the index, so you may feel that it is not worth the fee to read or buy them. You can obtain a copy of the grant for

Old photographs tend to depict important occasions such as weddings.

no extra charge, provided it is ordered at the same time as the will. The most recent indexes are less detailed than earlier ones, so the grant might contain vital clues about the relationships of the administrators to the deceased.

Indexes can be consulted at the Principal Registry of the Family Division at First Avenue House in London, which is open from 10 am to 4 pm on Monday to Friday only. District Probate Registries around the country also have copies of the indexes, though not for all years, and microfilm or microfiche copies can be found in some record offices and libraries, but again, not for all years. To read a will or admon incurs a small charge (£5 in 2003), which covers both the will and the grant, if you order them at the same time. There is a wait of about an hour while the document is scanned and sent to the search room for you. The copy is yours to take away. If you do not need the copy on the same day, and do not want to spend an extra hour in the search room, you can simply order a copy to be sent to you for the same fee, which takes about a week. You can also order copies by post, for the same fee, from the Postal Searches and Copies Department in York. They will also do a search of up to four years if you do not know the date of probate or administration, and do not have access to any copies of the indexes. If you require a longer search, an additional fee is payable. You can find more information on the Court Service website at **www.courtservice.gov.uk**. The *Family and*

Local History Handbook includes addresses of the District Registries and details of the indexes they hold. There are plans to put the probate indexes online and to make it possible to order wills on the internet.

The records in the PRFD are for England and Wales, but contain references to Scottish and Irish wills where there was some property in England and Wales. For these wills you should apply to the relevant office in Scotland or Ireland. The PRFD also has wills of people who died abroad, but were normally resident in England or Wales, and these can alert you to deaths which do not appear in the GRO indexes. It is often a good idea to look for a will as a short cut to finding a death certificate, since the will indexes are in annual, not quarterly volumes, making searching much quicker. The amount of detailed information in the index entries can be a great help in identifying the right individual, especially where the name is common. The nineteenth-century indexes are more detailed, but even the later ones include the full name and address of the deceased, the date of death and the date of probate.

Before 1858, proving wills was regarded as being a responsibility of the Church of England as a will was supposed to be a contract between the maker and God. Wills are thus not to be found in just one location. Surviving records – the earliest dating from the fifteenth century – are at a number of county record offices and some are at the Family Records Centre. Probate records before 1733 may be in Latin, but staff will help you to read them.

Records of wills proved at archdeacons' and diocesan courts, the least important places to prove wills, are held by local record offices. Archbishop's courts granted probate if there was property in two or more dioceses. There were two archbishop's courts, the Prerogative Court of York (PCY) which covered England north of the River Trent, and the Prerogative Court of Canterbury (PCC) for the rest of England and Wales. PCY records are at the Borthwick Institute of Historical Research in York.

If property was held both north and south of the Trent then property was proved in the Prerogative Court of Canterbury. The PCC also had jurisdiction over the estates of those who died abroad. Executors often had wills proved in courts higher than necessary. During the first half of the nineteenth century there was a growing tendency to use the PCC for even relatively small estates. There are a number of indexes to PCC wills – at the National

Archives, the Family Records Centre, the Society of Genealogists and elsewhere.

The important PCC records have been microfilmed and are available both at the Family Records Centre and at the NA. Some classes of material are just at the National Archives in Kew. There are surname indexes for most PCC wills, and eventually both the indexes and digitised images of the wills themselves will be found as part of PRO-Online at **www.pro-online.pro.gov.uk**. Wills are continually being added to the site, working back from 1858. In 2003, it included most PCC wills back to around 1750. The index is free, but there is a charge for downloading the images (£3 in 2003).

Poor Law

The phrases 'poor law' and 'union workhouse' conjure up visions of Victorian England, and of *Oliver Twist* in particular. The system, so vividly described by Charles Dickens, survived well into the twentieth century. Boards of Guardians were not abolished until 1930, and the Poor Law under which they had been formed lasted until 1948.

What was known as the New Poor Law was introduced in 1834, when parishes were grouped together into poor law unions. These new units were responsible for looking after all the poor or destitute people (paupers) in the constituent parishes. A workhouse was built in each union, and a number of officials were appointed to administer the system, headed by a Board of Guardians. Their principal duty was to relieve the poor, but over the years many other functions were added, many of which we would now associate with local government or the health service.

Relief usually took the form of admitting individuals and families to the workhouse, known as 'indoor relief', rather than disbursing sums to people who remained in their own homes, that is 'outdoor relief'. This was normally only given when the circumstances were likely to be temporary, such as an accident to the breadwinner, or to wives and children of men who were absent for some reason, serving in the armed forces or in prison, for example.

Men and women were housed separately in the workhouse, although families could be permitted to visit each other. The exceptions to this were children under seven who were allowed to stay with their mothers in the women's ward, and elderly infirm married couples who were allowed to stay together and were housed separately from the other inmates.

As well as the regular inmates in the workhouse, there were also the casual wards, where destitute tramps could be given one or two nights' board and lodging in return for some work. Most workhouses had their own sick wards or infirmaries, which were often used by the surrounding population as well as the inmates. Many of today's district general hospitals started out as workhouse infirmaries, and can often be identified by their distinctive Victorian gothic architecture. Unions also ran a network of asylums where pauper lunatics were to be sent, and some unions ran their own schools for pauper children.

Most poor law records are to be found in local record offices and libraries, and some are at the National Archives. These records cover an amazingly wide range of subjects, although they are mostly concerned with administrative matters and do not contain lists of names. Having said that, there remains a vast array of material which can help the family historian.

First of all there are records relating to the many staff who worked for the union in a wide variety of jobs. Each union appointed a medical officer and a chaplain, and from 1853 had responsibility for enforcing the Vaccination Act throughout the

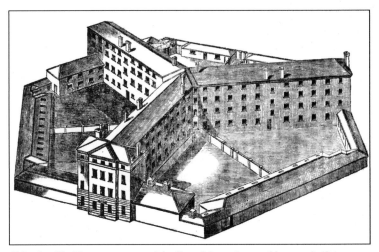

Abingdon Workhouse was one of the first of the union workhouses, built in the 1830s. The workhouse system was still in operation well into the twentieth century.

union, so a Vaccination Officer would be appointed. In the workhouse itself, the establishment was headed by a master and mistress, often a married couple, and other staff might include nursing staff, porters, attendants, bakers, tailors, clerks and teachers. The National Archives has registers of employees in series MH 9.

Far outnumbering the employees of the union were, of course, the paupers and inmates themselves. There is a range of records that can be used to find out more about these unfortunate men and women. An excellent set of guides compiled by Jeremy Gibson, Colin Rogers and Cliff Webb, called *Poor Law Union Records,* gives brief details of the surviving records for each poor law union, and where they can be found. At local record offices you might find admission and discharge registers, minute books, creed registers noting the religious denomination of workhouse inmates, orders for maintenance under the Bastardy Act of 1845, salary books for workhouse staff, and registers of births, baptisms and deaths in the workhouse. There might be some correspondence about individual paupers (and employees) in the correspondence between individual unions and Somerset House in series MH 12 at the National Archives.

One of the underlying principles since Elizabethan times was that everyone belonged to a particular parish where they were said to have a settlement. From 1834 the union was the place of settlement. If someone applied to the parish for poor relief, and on examination it could be proved that their place of settlement was elsewhere, they could be physically removed to their home parish, even if they had left it many years previously. There are surprising numbers of records about this, as unions and parishes were very keen to get rid of paupers who did not belong there.

Hospitals

Hospital records are not often used in family history research, but may have a good deal to offer us. Records containing clinical information will usually be closed for 100 years, but admission and discharge registers will not usually be subject to such restrictions. Many hospitals started as Poor Law Union infirmaries, and their records will usually be found in the appropriate county record office with the rest of the records for the union. Others were originally charitable or voluntary foundations. Again their records may also be at the county record office. Many hospitals retain their own records, and may have their own archivist: St Bartholomew's Hospital in London is an example of this. Fortunately there is now a quick way to locate the surviving records for any hospital in Great Britain, using the HOSPREC database compiled by the Wellcome Trust and the National Archives at **www.hospitalrecords.pro.gov.uk**.

Occupations

Although you cannot always expect to find detailed records of everyone's employment history, it may be worth investigating a little to see if any were kept, and if they survive. Occupational indexes exist for some trades, containing details of individual tradesmen. Their scope and completeness varies. A comprehensive list of these indexes appeared in the March 2003 issue of *Family History Monthly*.

If your ancestors worked for large organisations such as the railways or the Post Office, there may well be records of their employment. You will find an extensive collection of material relating to Post Office employees at Heritage Royal Mail, Freeling House, Phoenix Place, London WC1X 0DL, which welcomes researchers. There is more information on their website at **www.royalmailgroup.com/heritage**. Many records of railway employees can be found at the National Archives at Kew and elsewhere. The NA also has records of the members of the Metropolitan Police, since this force comes directly under the jurisdiction of the Home Office. Records for other police forces are rather patchy, but they can sometimes be found at local record offices.

You may also be in luck if an ancestor worked for a large company. Unfortunately you may not know who their employer was, only their occupation, so if someone was a weaver in a town full of mills, there is little point in looking any further. If you do know the employer, a good way of finding out where surviving records are to be found is through the National Register of Archives (NRA) – a database of information about the location of records in record offices and archives all over Britain. This can be checked on their website **www.hmc.gov.uk** and they welcome visitors to their reading room currently in London. However, the NRA is to become

Strike Bulletin

An Illustrated Summary of the News and Views to Date.

Published by Photochrom Co., Ltd., London and Tunbridge Wells

No. 1.   **SUNDAY, 9th MAY, 1926**   **Price 6d.**

POLICY.

THE STRIKE BULLETIN is to give the public an Illustrated Souvenir of recent events, and to fill as best it can, the gap caused by the suspension of the Illustrated papers and the pictures in the Dailies. Whether it will continue as a publication very properly depends on the development of the next few days. When the other illustrated papers resume it will depart from the scene, feeling grateful that no cause remains for its continued existence.

If, however, contrary to the best hopes, the feeling is expressed that publication should be continued, every effort will be made to carry on.

This past week has seen an eventful happening—the birth of two new daily papers, The British Gazette on Wednesday last, followed by The Workers' Gazette issued the following day.

The 'Strike Bulletin' is now published to shew pictures and to summarise the position up to the time of going to press.

The 'Strike Bulletin' is non-partisan, but desires to give the public some details in news and pictures, and to express the hope that wise counsels may prevail and that the big men of both sides will get together and prove their bigness by their ability to find a way out of the present difficulties on the principle of peace with honour.

HOW THE CARS WERE PARKED.—Miles of cars were parked in this way in all the principal London thoroughfares.   *Topical Press*

You may not find the names of your ancestors in the newspapers, but you can easily find accounts of events they might have taken part in or been affected by, such as the General Strike of 1926.

part of the National Archives in 2003 and shortly after will move to the Kew site. The records may not be where you would expect to find them. For instance, if you are looking for records of some London department stores, they may be in the archives of the University of Glasgow, which holds the records of the Glasgow-based House of Fraser Group, which includes such well-known stores as Dickins & Jones of Regent Street. Company records rarely include staff registers or other details of employees, although surviving company magazines and newspapers are often as informative.

If your ancestor belonged to a trade union, the NRA will also tell you which records survive and where they can be seen, although here again it is relatively uncommon for records of individual members to survive. The largest collection of trade union records is with the Modern Records Centre at the University of Warwick in Coventry. Its website suggests ways of finding out more about particular trades and professions. It can be found at: **www.warwick.ac.uk/services/library/mrc/index.shtml**.

Merchant seamen

Most records relating to merchant seamen are to be found at the National Archives, although if you are interested in the ships your ancestor sailed on, the National Maritime Museum is probably the best place to start. Unfortunately records about these seamen are very patchy, particularly for the nineteenth century, and can be difficult to use. The National Archives produces a series of leaflets that explain these records in more detail. In addition there are several excellent and comprehensive books about tracing merchant seamen, which are well worth buying (see page 182).

The earliest records date from 1747, when ships' musters and log books had to be kept, and they include lists of crew members. Unfortunately, few early log books survive – those that do are in series BT 98. Seamen registered with the Board of Trade between 1835 and 1857 and these records are in various series between BT 112 and BT 120. Details of seamen between 1858 and 1912 are found in the agreements and crew lists for individual ships – the National Archives has a 10 per cent sample. The largest collection of these records is in Canada with the Maritime History Archive, Memorial University of Newfoundland, St John's, Newfoundland A1B 3Y1,

Two brothers pose proudly for a photograph to send to their mother during the First World War.

www.mun.ca/mha with some others at the NMM or in local record offices. There are also numerous other short-lived series of records between 1835 and 1913, which may provide information. It certainly helps to know the individual's rank and his specialism (engineer, deck hand, mate) before you start looking.

Service records for those who served in the Merchant Navy during the First World War are virtually non-existent. Unfortunately, record cards from the Central Index Register covering the period 1913 to 1920, were destroyed some time ago. All that survives are the cards from a special index for 1918 to 1921. Each card usually gives name, place and date of birth, a short description and a photograph of the man.

The Central Index Register of Seamen between 1921 and 1941, which is available on microfiche in the Microfilm Reading Room at the National Archives, includes details of all categories of people (men and women) employed at sea, not just ordinary seamen, but also mates, engineers, trimmers, stewards, cooks, etc. The surviving cards are unusual in that they usually include a photograph of the individual, together with a date and place of birth, rating, a brief description and a list of ships served on. The more recent Central Register of Seamen from 1942 to 1972 comprises docket books and seamen's pouches in series BT 373 and BT 382. The books contain an entry for each seafarer and are arranged alphabetically under several headings. The pouches contain records relating to an individual seaman. The contents can cover the period 1913–72.

Lloyd's Captains' Registers gives the main information on foreign-going masters and mates between 1851 and 1947. The registers are kept at Guildhall Library in London, with an incomplete set of microfilm copies at the NA. There are also Certificates of Competency and Service (to 1921). Successful applications for these certificates (before 1928) are held by the National Maritime Museum.

Merchant seamen who lost their lives during the two World Wars are commemorated in rolls of honour in BT 339. Other deaths (for passengers as well), marriages and births at sea are recorded in BT 334 (1871–1992) with earlier records in BT 158 and BT 160. These records are described in a leaflet from the NA, *Births, Marriages and Deaths at Sea*. This is one of many information leaflets available from the NA or via its website **www.pro.gov.uk**.

Men of the Mercantile Marine Reserve, and officers and men of the Royal Naval Reserve, received the 1914–15 Star (if they had seen service before the end of 1915), the British War Medal and the Victory Medal. The Mercantile Marine War Medal (NMVM) was awarded to those with sea service of not less than six months between 4 August 1914 and 11 November 1918, and who served at sea on at least one voyage through a danger zone. All those who received the MMWM medal were then automatically entitled to receive the British War Medal. For merchant seamen, the National Maritime Museum has returns of deaths, 1914–19; and at the NA there are the Registers of Deceased Seamen, 1914–18 (BT 334/62, 65, 67, 71 and 73).

Schools

Since the Education Act of 1870, when schooling was made compulsory, schools have been required to keep records of their pupils. As well as the daily attendance register, there was also an admission and discharge register. As each new pupil joined the school, their details would be recorded in the register. Each child's entry consists of a single line, starting with their name, address and birth date, together with the name of their parent or guardian, and sometimes their occupation too. Then the school would add the date the child started at the school, and the name of the last school they attended, if any. During their school career a brief note would be made of the educational standards attained and, when they finally left, the reason for leaving would be given. If the child transferred to another school, or moved out of the area, their destination might be given, provided that this was known.

This information can be invaluable in tracing the movements of your ancestors and establishing precisely when a family moved from one area to another. Not only that, it can be a good way of finding members of a family, since brothers and sisters are likely to have attended the same school. In addition these registers can help locate the birth of an individual ancestor if he or she has a very common name. For example, you may know where your John Smith was born, and in what year, though not the exact date. If you know his father's name and occupation, which you should find on his marriage certificate, you can consult the admission and discharge register for the school he is likely to have attended. His entry will provide the exact date of birth.

Not all registers survive, but most are deposited in county record offices, or local studies libraries, although some may still be with the school. If you do not know the name of the school your ancestor attended, there are several ways you can find out the most likely one. He or she probably attended the one nearest their home, so you can look at a large-scale Ordnance Survey map of the right date to find out. In smaller towns and villages there will be fewer to choose from, so you may be able to work it out from the name of the place alone. Details of local schools are often provided in street or trade directories. However, if they went to a religious school (particularly Catholic ones) they may have travelled further afield, as did any older children who attended a grammar school.

There may also be school log books and punishment books. Log books are reports of the day-to-day happenings in a school and are very useful as a way of building up an idea of an ancestor's schooling, although they may never be mentioned by name. Records such as punishment books, which contain sensitive personal information, may be closed for 70 years or more.

Although most people will have attended the maintained schools, a substantial minority did not. If your ancestors were in the workhouse, their children may have attended a workhouse school. The records of these schools are mostly to be found in county record offices, where they will be found with the other Poor Law Union material. The information contained in the registers is similar to those of the maintained schools. The children were

```
            EXAMINATION RESULTS.
            - - - - - - - - - - - - - - - -

December, 1939.    Oxford School Certificates.
                   - - - - - - - - - - - - - - - -

1.  Betty Fruin.    Passed in English Language(C),
                    Shakespeare(C), English History(C),
                    British Empire History, Art(C),
                    Geography(C), and Book-keeping(C).

2.  George Loosemore. Eng. Lang. (C), Brit. Emp. Hist.,
                    Geography(A), French, Art(C), and
                    Woodwork(A).

3.  Hugh Beaumont.  Eng. Lang.(C), Brit. Emp. Hist.,
                    Geography(C), Mathematics(C), Biology,
                    and Book-keeping(C).


March, 1940.       The Royal Society of Arts.

English, Stage 2   2nd Class. T.Lawlor, L.Pickett.
        1st. Class. P.Cole, V.Huggins.
Stage I.            A.Horniblow, A.Payne, J.Jordan,
                    S.White, D.Emanuel, K.Fall, B.Pegg,
                    J.Langford(Credit) P.Mourton,
                    W.Lowry, J.Townsend, G.Tanner(Cred.),
                    H.Hunt, D.Thompson, D.Obey.

Arithmetic Stage 1. D.Emanuel, D.Read, I.Norris,
                    I.Knowles, J.Townsend, W.Argent,
                    S.Stallion.

French, Stage 1.    A.Horniblow, L.Pickett.
```

This old school magazine from Loughborough Central School, Brixton, is full of names and details about school life for evacuees from London in the early days of the Second World War. As well as giving a vivid picture of what life was like for the children, told in their own words, it is full of names which can be followed up in other sources, such as the school's admission and discharge registers.

mostly foundlings or orphans, or without parents or close relatives able to take care of them, and if you are lucky the records may contain extra information about how they came to be in the care of the Poor Law authorities in the first place. When the children were old enough to leave school the union may have placed them in apprenticeships or employment and, again, there may be a record of this.

At the other end of the social scale are the fee-paying schools, the more exclusive of them confusingly called public schools. Many of them, especially the public schools, have printed registers of former pupils, and these may be consulted in large reference

Make sure you keep notes of all the details you can think of. Background details, such as the pictures and piano in this 1930s classroom, are wonderful for stirring memories in older relatives.

libraries. The Society of Genealogists' Library has a particularly good collection of registers and school histories. The amount of detail contained in the registers varies but may give the name and occupation of the pupil's father and their home address. As with the maintained schools, there is a good chance that other members of the family attended the same school, and this may extend over several generations. A further bonus is that each pupil's entry may include details of their career after leaving the school, although this will depend on the pupil or their family having provided the information. This may include attendance at a university, or details of entry into a profession or the armed services. Some schools also produced a roll of honour of former pupils who served in the World Wars, which may give similar biographical information, and may even include photographs. Some of the older schools may even have their own archives, which could provide further information on former pupils, although more recent records may not be open to inspection.

For the very small number of men (and even smaller numbers of women) who went on to university, there are often published lists of former students. The best known of these are for England's two ancient universities, *Alumni Oxonienses* for Oxford and *Alumni Cantabrigienses* for Cambridge. Both of these are in print, and the

Alumni Cantabrigienses 1261–1900 is also available on the internet at **www.ancestry.co.uk**, which can be accessed for a fee, while *Alumni Oxonienses* 1500–1886 can be purchased on CD-Rom. Both Oxford and Cambridge are made up of colleges, and each of them has its own alumni register, which is usually more detailed than the general university list, so you may want to check this when you have found out which college your ancestor attended. Other universities produced similar lists. Again the best collection of this material is at the Society of Genealogists.

Apprentices

Until fairly recently the only way to learn a trade or occupation was to become an apprentice and serve an agreed period with a master. For many employers, apprentices were little more than cheap labour – which is why legal documents, called indentures, were drawn up and signed which set out the obligations on both the master and the apprentice. The survival of these indentures is

If you have original documents in your collection, make sure they are safely and securely stored.

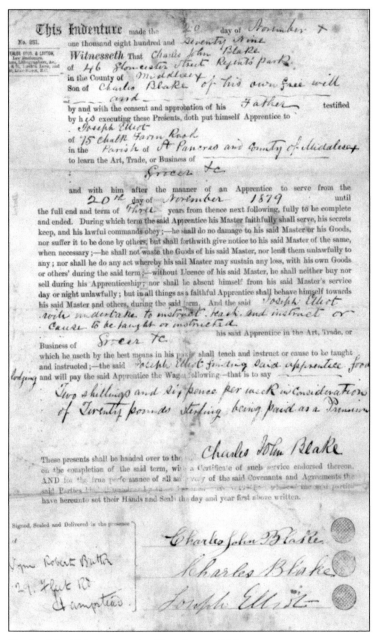

Charles John Blake's apprenticeship indenture, 1879.

patchy. The Society of Genealogists (SoG) has a small collection and many can also be found at local record offices, particularly in parish and poor law records as many orphans and poor children were indentured to learn a trade. Livery companies in the City of London also arranged the apprenticeship of many children to trades, and these records are either with Guildhall Library in London, or with the company itself. The Goldsmiths' Company has a particularly fine collection.

There is no national index of apprentices. The nearest that there is are the tax records which were kept between 1710 and 1811, which list names and trades of masters and apprentices and the dates of their indenture. These records are at the National Archives (in series IR 1), with copies of an index between 1710 and 1774 at both the NA and the SoG. The records are by no means complete, as there was much evasion and many exemptions were granted.

Newspapers

There can be few individuals who have not appeared in a local or even a national newspaper over the years. From the middle of the nineteenth century, most towns had at least one local newspaper. They can be very useful in your research, although people can be put off by the sheer amount of information available. Details of some local newspapers can be found in *Local Newspapers 1750–1920, A Select Location List,* by Jeremy Gibson, Brett Langston and Brenda Smith, which also indicates whether there are any indexes.

Copies of most national and local newspapers (as well as magazines and periodicals) are available at the British Library Newspaper Library at Colindale, north-west London and are listed on their website **http://prodigi.bl.uk/nlcat**. If you know the date and place of an event, it is easy to locate the paper it is likely to have been reported in, using the Newspaper Library Catalogue. You can also use the catalogue to search for newspapers and periodicals on particular subjects. Copies of local newspapers (usually on microfilm) are also often found in local record offices and libraries. Local studies libraries may have collections of cuttings, which are often well indexed. In the past (as in the present) readers liked to hear about other people's misfortunes, so crime, scandal and grisly accidents were always likely to be reported.

There is likely to be coverage of events such as sporting occasions, charity dinners and council meetings. These will include lists of names, and your ancestor may be one of them, although you may have a very long search unless you know that he or she was involved on a particular occasion. If you have a death certificate which indicates a sudden or untimely death, there will usually have been an inquest, and the date and place of this will appear on the death certificate. A report of the proceedings will probably appear, often in great detail in the case of murders: this may be more informative than is provided in the coroner's records themselves. If there is more than one local paper, you should check them all, if possible, because details may vary between papers.

Many papers have regular birth, marriage and death columns, so you may find your ancestor's death notice in one of these. This may not provide any details you have not already seen on the death certificate, but some entries include the place of burial, which can otherwise be a very difficult piece of information to find. A few papers even published weekly lists of interments in the local cemeteries. If your ancestor was of some prominence in the community, there may even be an obituary, or a detailed report of his or her funeral. Deaths of servicemen were frequently reported in local papers during the First World War, often accompanied by a photograph.

Crime has always been a popular subject and court proceedings of various kinds may be reported, sometimes verbatim. If you do not know when and where a trial took place, and the crime was of sufficient magnitude, the index to *The Times* may help.

The advertisements may also be useful. If your ancestor owned a business, even on a small scale, this might have had to be sold when he or she died, if no member of the family was able to carry it on, so a notice to this effect might appear soon after the person died. If they were declared bankrupt, this could also be the reason for a sale. There may also have been regular or occasional advertisements for the business, especially if he or she ran a shop, or dealt directly with the public in some other way. Photographers, insurance agents and brewers are just a few of those who regularly advertised their services.

Unfortunately there are very few indexes to individual newspapers, so the chances of finding the report of an event without knowing the date and place may not be good. The best known of all the national papers, *The Times,* has however been indexed and these indexes are now available on CD-Rom in a few libraries, including the National Archives. The printed indexes can be found in many libraries, which may also have microfilm copies of *The Times* itself. There are four volumes a year. *The Times* often includes stories about local court cases and the like in the London area, so it is not uncommon for ordinary people to appear within its pages.

Printed biographical sources

You might be pleasantly surprised to find how many of your ancestors appeared in printed sources. Many people are listed in directories relating to their trade or profession, such as the Institute of Electrical Engineers or the Royal Statistical Society. Members of both Houses of Parliament can be found in the annual *Dod's Parliamentary Companion,* which may include short biographies and even photographs. Annual directories of the legal and medical professions and the clergy have been published annually since the nineteenth century or even earlier. *Crockford's* and the *Clerical Directory,* for example, list Anglican clergy: each entry shows a summary of his career, with dates of ordination and of all the posts held in the Church. They also include his current address and the titles of any books he may have written. The *Law List* contains similar information about barristers and solicitors. The medical profession is similarly dealt with in publications such as the *Medical Register* and the *Medical Directory.* From these directories of professions it is possible to outline a person's career. Large reference libraries and the National Archives and Society of Genealogists libraries have substantial collections of these books.

There is also a variety of almanacs and yearbooks with lists of names, such as the *British Imperial Calendar,* the *Civil Service Year Book* and the *Foreign Office* and *Colonial Office Lists.* Some do not contain biographical details (except perhaps for senior managers), but list office holders at that time. However, by going through them year by year it is still possible to construct the outline of a career. Many government office holders are listed in an online database at **www.ihrinfo.ac.uk/office**.

Apart from contemporary sources like almanacs and directories, there are many printed works that are compilations of information about members of particular occupational or social groups. These

THE LONDON COUNTY COUNCIL.
SPRING GARDENS, S.W.

List of Aldermen and Councillors.

Chairman, Dr. W. J. Collins, J.P.
Vice-Chairman, R. M. Beachcroft.
Deputy-Chairman, A. M. Torrance.

NAME.	ELECTORAL DIVISION.	NAME.	ELECTORAL DIVISION.
Abrahams, M.	Whitechapel.	Cooper, G. J.	Bermondsey.
Antrobus, R. C., J.P.	8 George, Hanover Sq.	Corbett, T. L., J.P.	Clapham.
		Cornwall, E. A., J.P.	Fulham.
Arnold, Sir Arthur	*Alderman till 1898.*	Costelloe, B. F. C.	Chelsea.
		Crooks, William	Poplar.
Baker, J. A.	East Finsbury.	Davies, W., J.P.	Battersea.
Banning, H. T.	Greenwich.	Denbigh, Earl of	City of London.
Bayley, Edric.	W. Southwark.	Hayter, L. H.	Westminster.
Beachcroft, R. M.	*Alderman till 1898.*	Dickinson, W. H.	*Alderman till 1898.*
Benn, J. W	East Finsbury.	Dimsdale, Sir J. C.	City of London.
Bicker-Caarten, G.	Mile End.	Dixon, J.	Kennington.
Blake, W. F.	Cent. Finsbury.	Dudley, Earl of.	Holborn.
Bond, Edward, M.P.	Hampstead.	Dumphreys, J. M. T.	Deptford.
Boulnois, E., M.P.	E. Marylebone.	Dunraven, Earl of, K.P.	Wandsworth.
Branch, James, J.P.	S. W. Bethnal Green.	Ellice-Clark, E. B.	North Hackney.
		Elliott, G. S.	S. Islington.
Bruce, W. W.	Bow & Bromley.	Emden, T. W. L., J.P.	Strand.
Bull, W. J.	Hammersmith.	Fardell, T. G., M.P.	S. Paddington.
Burns, John, M.P.	Battersea.	Farquhar, Sir H. B. T.,	
Campbell, C. H., J.P.	S. Kensington.	Bt., M.P.	E. Marylebone.
Campbell, Col. F.	Norwood.	Farrer, Lord	*Alderman till 1901.*
Carrington, Earl	W. St. Pancras.		
Chapman, C. M.	Chelsea.	Fletcher, J. S., J.P	Hampstead.
Clarke, Henry	City of London.	Ford, Lieut.-Col. C.	N. Lambeth.
Cohen, B. L., M.P.	City of London.	Forman, E. Baxter	N. Hackney.
Collins, W. J., M.D., J.P.	W. St. Pancras.	Fox, W. H.	N. Kensington.
Cooper, Benjamin	Bow & Bromley.	Freak, Charles	N.E.BethnalGn.

Printed sources such as almanacs may list names of officials, such as local councillors, civil servants and members of the judiciary. This example is from the Sunlight Year Book of 1898.

include titles such as *Burke's Peerage, Debrett's Peerage* and a whole range of biographical dictionaries. Burke's and Debrett's are the best known of this kind of work, although Burke's is the more detailed of the two. It includes details of the births, marriages and deaths not just of peers of the realm, but of their whole families, including younger sons, so the range of individuals mentioned is perhaps wider than might be supposed. However, these peerage books are not the only ones of their kind, and *Burke's Landed Gentry of Great Britain and Ireland* lists pedigrees of wealthy landed families who did not have hereditary titles. *Walford's County Families of the United Kingdom* covers similar ground in various editions between 1860 and the Second World War. *Kelly's Handbook to the Titled, Landed and Official Classes* was published annually from 1874 with brief biographical details of the heads of families. The Society of Genealogists and the British Library have the largest collection of these books, but they can also be found in many other libraries.

Biographical dictionaries may cover a very wide range of people indeed. The most important and comprehensive of these is *The Dictionary of National Biography,* which was first published in 1885. There have been several supplements, and 2004 is the publication date of a completely revised edition. In it can be found essays on the lives of distinguished public figures, artists, writers, politicians, clerics and the occasional eccentric. The entries vary in length, some covering several pages. Many other biographical dictionaries have been published over the years, some of them dedicated to specific groups such as writers, women or the labour movement, to name but a few. Even professional footballers are the subject of a series of volumes compiled by the Association of Football Statisticians. A very useful resource is the *British Biographical Archive,* a compilation of 168,000 entries from a wide range of biographical dictionaries. This is available on microfiche in two series, with a composite index in book form. It has proved very useful in locating information on relatively minor figures who do not appear in more general works.

Who's Who has been published annually since 1897. It includes entries only on living people, containing information supplied by the individuals themselves, covering their parentage, education, marriage and career. The entries of those who have died have been published as *Who Was Who* at intervals, and the latest version is now available on CD-Rom. The *Who's Who* format has been borrowed by other publishers of works dedicated to specific areas such as the theatre, or architecture, for example.

Many of these volumes can be found in large reference libraries or at the Society of Genealogists in London.

Directories

The first trade directories were published in the late eighteenth century, but are more comprehensive and useful from around 1850. Directories vary in format, but generally cover a whole county or a large city. London directories, for example, are usually arranged into the following sections:

- a trade section with the names of persons engaged in each trade
- an alphabetical list of people together with their occupations

situated in a valley, and approached through an avenue of lime trees; the park and woods of this estate extend over an area of 5,000 acres; George III. visited here in 1804 and 1805; it is the property and residence of Everard Alex. Hambro esq. D.L. J.P. who is lord of the manor and sole landowner. The soil is chalk; subsoil, chalk. The area is 4,872 acres of land and 8 of water; rateable value, £3,253; the population in 1901 was 650 in the civil, and 677 in the ecclesiastical parish.

By a Local Government Board Order, dated March 25, 1882, a detached part of this parish, known as Lyscombe, was amalgamated with Cheselbourne and at the same date another detached part, known as Holworth, was added to Overmoigne in the Weymouth union, and by the Divided Parishes Act a detached part of Winterborne Whitchurch was added to Milton Abbas.

Parish Clerk, Henry Fookes.

(Marked thus * receive their letters via Milborne St. Andrew.)

PRIVATE RESIDENTS.

Fielding Thomas M.D
Fookes Henry, The Brewery
Fookes William, Rose cottage
Hambro Everard Alex. D.L., J.F. Milton abbey
Mears Rev. Edward M.A. (curate)
Pentin Rev. Herbert M.A. (vicar), Vicarage
Yates Robert, Hill house

COMMERCIAL.

Adams Robert John, Hambro Arms hotel & posting house
*Almer Joseph, farmer, Bagber & Long Ash farms
Ancient Order of Foresters (W. Guy, secretary)
Best Charles, organist at the Abbey & parish church
Bussell Wm. shoe maker & dairyman

Clark Alfred C. schoolmaster
Cottage Hospital (Thos. Fielding M.D. medical officer; Rev. H. Pentin M.A. chaplain; R. Yates, hon. sec. & treas.; Nurse Ashford, matron)
Evans Walter Holtiff, registered shoeing smith & agricultural implement agent & repairer
Flander Thomas, carrier
Fielding Thos. M.D. surgeon, & medical officer & public vaccinator, 3rd district, Blandford union & 3rd district, Cerne union
Fookes Bros. (old established), wholesale & family brewers, maltsters & wine & spirit merchants
Foster Joph. farmer, East Luccombe
Guy Albert, blacksmith
Guy James, carrier
Guy William, estate clerk, assistant overseer & clk. to the Parish Council
Jeans Thomas, Milton Arms P.H
Keynes Thos. farmer, Chescombe frm
Lovell Frank, carpenter

Sexton, Frank Lovell.
Post, M. O. & T. O., T. M. O., S. B., E. D., P. P. & A. & I. O.—Miss Lauretta Vatcher, sub-postmistress. Letters are received through Blandford at 6.45 a.m. & 2.40 p.m.; & are dispatched at 12.35 & 6.30 p.m.; sundays, 11.30 a.m

Elementary School (mixed), with master's residence attached, built in 1840, for 150 children; average attendance, 62; Alfred C. Clark, master; Mrs. Annie Clark, mistress

Carriers to :
Blandford—Thomas Flander, mon. & fri. & James Guy, thurs. & sat.
Dorchester—Thomas Flander, wed. & sat.; & James Guy, tues. & fri

Marlow Elizabeth(Mrs.), grocer & drps
Milton Abbas Football Club (Walter Holtiff Evans, sec)
Parsons Hy. & Sons, grocers & bakers
Perkins Charles, head gardener to E. A. Hambro esq
Reading Room & Library (Walter Holtiff Evans, sec)
Rogers William John, shoe maker & dairyman, Dale cottage
Shuler Charles, woodman to E. A. Hambro esq
Snook William, farmer, Barnes hill
Spiller Thos. Robt. frmr. Luccombe, hm
Stokes William, farm bailiff to E. A. Hambro esq. Delcombe
Tett Sarah (Mrs.), miller, Milton mill
Vatcher Lauretta (Miss), grcr. Post off
*Warren Frederick, farmer, Hewish
Wright Walter, head gamekeeper to E. A. Hambro esq
Wrixon Joseph Knight,frmr. Long close
Yates Robert, agent to E. A. Hambro esq. Milton Abbey Estate office

MINTERNE MAGNA is a village and parish, extending 4 miles, in the Western division of the county, liberty of Pydeltrenthide, petty sessional division and union of Cerne, Dorchester county court district, rural deanery of Whitchurch (Cerne portion), archdeaconry of Dorset and diocese of Salisbury. The village is about 1 mile west of the road from Dorchester to Crewkerne, 5 miles east from Evershot station at Holywell, on the Weymouth branch of the Great Western railway, 10 north from Dorchester and about 2 north from Cerne. The church of St. Andrew is a plain building of stone, in the Gothic style, consisting of chancel, nave, and an embattled western tower with pinnacles, containing a clock and 5 tubular bells; the chancel and north aisle were restored by the late H. C. Sturt esq.: in 1804 the tower was restored and heightened, and in 1897 the church was entirely reseated in oak and a stained window erected as memorials to the late Hon. Theresa Digby: there is also a memorial window, erected in 1866, to Lady Caroline Karrison: there are 170 sittings. The register dates from the year 1695. The living is a rectory, net income £82, with 5 acres of glebe and residence, in the gift of Lord Alington, of Mors Crichel, and held since 1887 by the Rev. William George Barclay, of Downing College, Cambridge. Charities amounting to £4 10s. yearly, derived from the gifts of Sir N. Napier and Sir H. Digby, are expended in coal for the aged poor; the Shebas Kent benefaction of £6 13s. yearly, is expended as approved by the owner of Minterne House and there is also a charity of £1 5s. yearly, left by the Rev. Henry Fix. Minterne House, the seat of Lord Digby J.P. is situated in the centre of the village, and nearly surrounded by a well-wooded park of 100 acres. The principal landowners are Lord Digby, who is lord of the manor, Lord Alington and Thomas Holford esq. of Castle Hill, Buckland Newton. The soil is clay; subsoil, gravel. The chief crops are corn, and there is much pasture land. The area is 2,204 acres of land and 2 of water; rateable value, £2,425; the population in 1901 was 306.

Hartley, 2 miles north-west; Lyons Gate, 1 mile north; and Middlemarsh, on the road from Dorchester to Crewkerne, 3 miles north and 6 miles south from Sherborne, are tithings; at the latter place is a Wesleyan chapel.

GOREWOOD, adjoining this parish on the north, was formerly extra-parochial, but is now a parish in the Cerne union, and was without population in 1901; its area is 51 acres; rateable value, £38.

Parish Clerk, John Clarke.

Post Office.—George Cheeseman, sub-postmaster. Letters arrive from Dorchester at 7.35 a.m. & 3 p.m. & are dispatched at 5.55 p.m. Postal Orders are issued & paid here. The nearest money order & telegraph office is at Cerne Abbas, 3 miles distant
Wall Letter Box, Lyons Gate, cleared at 5.30 p.m. week days only
Pillar Letter Box, Middlemarsh, cleared at 10 a.m. week days only
Elementary School (mixed), built in 1860, with residence for mistress, for 60 children; average attendance, 57; supported by Lord Digby; Mrs. Elizabeth Smith, mistress
Carrier.—Thomas Fox, from Cerne to Sherborne, passing through Minterne every thurs

MINTERNE MAGNA.

Digby Lord J.P. Minterne house; 39 Belgrave sq. & Guards', Travellers' & Carlton clubs, London S W
Barclay Rev. Wm. Geo. (rector), Rectry

COMMERCIAL.

Cheeseman Geo. carpenter, Post office
Cross William, jun. farmer & steward to Lord Digby, Manor farm
Curtis John, farmer, Highfield

Durden Emma (Mrs.), shopkeeper, Lyons gate
Durden Stephen, farmer, Lyons gate
Eavis Charles, farmer, Lyons gate
Foot Ellen (Mrs.), village nurse
Fox Aminda (Mrs.), farmer, Hartley
Knell Thomas, shoe maker,Lyons gate
Napier Timothy James, wood dealer, Lyons gate
Peacock Jn. gardener to Lord Digby
Summers Jas. gamekpr. to Lord Digby

MIDDLEMARSH.

(Letters arrive through Sherborne.)

COMMERCIAL.

Foot Nelson, farmer
Foot Philip, farmer
Gould James, farmer
Popham Edwin (Mrs.) farmer
Waygood Harry, farmer
Waygood James, farmer
Welch John, White Horse P.H

MONKTON WYLD is an ecclesiastical parish, formed in 1850 out of Whitchurch Canonicorum in Dorset and Uplyme in Devon; it is 4 miles south-east from Axminster station on the London and South Western railway, 3 north from Lyme Regis, 2½ north-west from Charmouth, and about 9 west from Bridport, in the Western division of the county, Bridport petty sessional division, union and county court district, Bridport rural deanery (Lyme portion), Dorset archdeaconry and Salisbury diocese. The part of the parish called Harcombe is in Devonshire; for civil purposes the parish was, by Local Government Board Order,on March 24,1884,transferred to Wootton Fitzpaine. The church of St. Andrew is a building of flint with stone dressings, in the Middle Pointed

Trade directories, such as this example from Kelly's of 1903, can be good sources for addresses and all kinds of useful information about the towns and villages where our ancestors lived.

- a classified alphabetical arrangement of streets, containing the names and occupations of tradespeople
- a Court Directory listing of the richer householders

County directories are similar, but do not usually have a street section, except perhaps for the largest towns.

Directories can be used to check whether ancestors were at a particular address, if they were in business of some kind. The names of all householders do not normally appear until around the First World War or later. It is important to remember that directories are often a year or two out of date, as it took some time to compile and publish them.

Many directories also include descriptions of towns and villages, with details of population, churches and chapels and local industries, which can provide useful (and interesting) background about the area in which an ancestor lived.

Most local studies libraries and county record offices have incomplete sets for their areas. The best collection covering the whole country is at Guildhall Library in London. The holdings of local studies libraries are described at **www.familia.org.uk**. Copies of directories are now widely available on microfiche and CD-Rom. In addition, the University of Leicester is making digitised images from many nineteenth-century directories available online at **www.historicaldirectories.org**, which can be quickly searched by name to find entries for an ancestor.

Telephone directories are also useful for checking addresses, although of course this relies on the individual having a phone. Ownership of telephones was reasonably rare before the 1950s. The most complete set of telephone books is held by the BT Group Archives in London.

Electoral registers

Since 1929, almost all adults in Britain have had the vote, and their names are recorded in electoral registers. These records can be useful to family history research, but there are a number of limitations. First of all, the lists are mostly in street order and not indexed by surname, so you need to know where a person lived to find them. Secondly, no women could vote in national elections before 1918, although some could vote in local elections, and until the same year only about 60 per cent of men had the vote. Even when the franchise was extended in 1918 to all men over 21, only women over 30 could vote at first. It was not until 1929 that the vote was finally given to all women over 21.

Despite these drawbacks, there are a number of uses that can be made of electoral registers. If you know where someone lived, you can use the register to see who else was resident at that address, and look at a series of registers to find out how long they lived there. As names of family members appear and disappear at an address over a number of years, it may be possible to build up a picture of the family, and use the information to search in other sources, depending on what you already know about them. For example, when a new member of the family appears, it may be that they have just reached voting age – 21 until 1967, then 18 – or perhaps a widowed parent has come to live with a married son or daughter. When a name disappears, it could be a clue to look for their death, or perhaps a grown-up son or daughter has left home to get married. Or a new name may belong to the spouse of the newly married son or daughter who has moved in with the family.

A standard listing in an electoral register gives no information about an individual but there may be a number of clues, depending on the period covered by it. These may indicate that a person was entitled to vote only in local or only in national elections. Service voters or merchant seamen may be indicated by 'S' or 'M'. From 1928, 'Y' indicates someone who will become eligible to vote in the first half of the year in which the register is in force, that is they will attain the age of 21, or 18 from 1967.

The date when a register was compiled may be significant. It takes a long time to compile and produce a register, so there is always a gap between the gathering of the information and its publication. For this reason a register gives a more accurate portrayal of who was living at a particular address a year or more before the date of the register.

Arrangements and qualifications for voting in local elections were originally quite different from parliamentary elections. County councils were established in 1889, and parish councils in 1894. There were separate elections and lists of electors for these, as well as elections to the workhouse board of guardians or the school board.

Nowadays, all adults are entitled to vote, unless they are disqualified for a specific reason such as bankruptcy. Peers, who have a vote in the House of Lords, cannot vote in parliamentary elections but may do so in local or European elections. In previous years there were a number of other exclusions, some of them surprising. Policemen and those who had left the force within the previous six months were not allowed to vote until 1887, and it was not until 1918 that disqualifications were removed from election agents, postmasters, most collectors of government revenues, and those in receipt of poor relief (including their spouses and children). First World War conscientious objectors were not allowed to vote until 1924. People serving a prison sentence, undischarged bankrupts and anyone convicted of bribery at a recent election are still disqualified from voting.

While property qualifications were in force up to 1919, the registers reflected this, with an indication of the nature of the qualification. Surprisingly, there may be more detail about lodgers, where the number of rooms they occupied may even be shown. Lodgers are usually listed separately from the main series of owners and occupiers, so you should check carefully how a register is laid out to be sure that you do not miss a section when you are searching.

Many registers are in county record offices or local studies libraries, and recent registers may still be with the local authority in the town or city hall. The British Library should have a copy of most registers from 1937 to the present, and may have others for earlier dates, although to see them you have to give four days' notice. There is a useful guide to the location of many registers, *Electoral Registers Since 1832; and Burgess Rolls* by Jeremy Gibson and Colin Rogers, unfortunately out of print, but reference libraries may have copies.

Some interesting pages about electoral registers and their history can be found at **www.bl.uk/services/information/spis_er.htm**.

Maps and pictures

Record offices, libraries and museums often have collections of photographs and prints for their area, some dating back many years. The local authority may have commissioned photographs of streets and buildings due to be demolished, and these may form part of a record office collection.

Maps can also be an important source for family history, less for finding out about individuals but as a way of building up a picture

Maps might be made for special purposes, such as this Second World War example showing the homes of Air Raid Precaution (ARP) Wardens and the positions of fire hydrants.

of where they lived. Ordnance Survey maps, in particular, are very valuable. They have been produced in a variety of scales for the last 200 years. The larger-scale maps can provide an astonishing level of detail about the streets and building where your family lived, even down to the location of the nearest post box. Record offices and local studies libraries should have maps of their own area. Some indeed may be annotated, for example showing where bombs fell during the Second World War or the location of pubs in 1910.

A number of old Ordnance Survey maps have been reprinted. David & Charles, for example, have reprinted the first series of one-inch maps, which give a picture of the countryside as the railways arrived, although the quality of reproduction is not always high. Alan Godfrey has reproduced large-scale late-nineteenth-century maps of many British towns. Most reference libraries or record offices sell his maps for their area or you can buy them from him directly at Alan Godfrey Maps, Prospect Business Park, Leadgate, Consett, Co. Durham, DH8 7PW or via **www.alangodfreymaps.co.uk**. It is also possible to download extracts from old maps on the internet or buy copies (which are rather more expensive than Alan Godfrey's) at **www.old-maps.co.uk**.

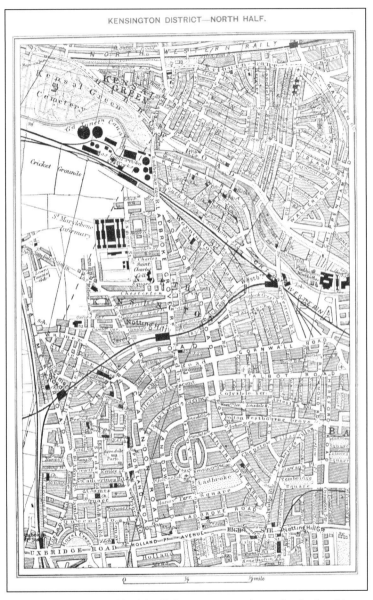

KENSINGTON DISTRICT—NORTH HALF.

Old maps provide a wealth of detail about an area, and can often be found in record offices and libraries. Many reprints of old Ordnance Survey maps have been published, and there are plenty of original old maps to be found on the second-hand market. This one is from a book published in 1903.

If your ancestor owned land in the late eighteenth century or early nineteenth century, there are several series of records in which they may appear. Enclosure maps (and accompanying schedules of property) record the rearrangement of land ownership which took place in many parishes (but certainly not all) between about 1660 and 1850. These are mainly to be found at local record offices. Tithe maps were drawn up after the Commutation of Tithes Act 1836 to show the ownership and occupants of land in every parish. Several copies of these maps were made and

An example of a field book showing details of the White Horse Inn at Middlemarsh, Dorset. This was part of the Valuation Office Survey made just before the First World War, popularly known as Lloyd George's Domesday.

normally one copy survives at the National Archives and another at the local record office.

A little-known source is the Valuation Office maps and books. The government conducted a survey, between 1910 and 1916, which tried to ascertain the value of every property in England and Wales. The maps are based on large-scale Ordnance Survey plans of the period, and the books contain a description of every house and the facilities it had. Both maps and books are at the National Archives, and leaflets are available explaining how to use these sometimes tricky, but very rewarding, records.

Immigration

Over the generations, hundreds of thousands of people have come to Britain – from the Huguenots (French Protestants) in the seventeenth century to the Ugandan Asians in the 1970s – to escape persecution or to seek to better themselves. There may be a family legend that an ancestor was born abroad or foreign origins may be suggested by the surname. Unfortunately, there was no requirement for immigrants to register with the authorities before 1905. The government's attitude was that everyone was welcome in Britain provided they caused no trouble. So it can be difficult to find out very much about them and where they came from.

The major source of information about migrants is the records relating to naturalisation and denization at the National Archives, which are well indexed and easy to use. Copies of the indexes can also be consulted at the Family Records Centre, although to see the documents themselves you will need to go to Kew. The records give a detailed account of the immigrant's background and place of origin, which may be just the information you need to extend your searches back to their country of origin. It's also worth checking the records of denization, a process that was less comprehensive than full naturalisation, and so was somewhat cheaper.

The authorities began to keep passenger lists in 1878 for ships which arrived in Britain from ports outside Europe and the Mediterranean. These lists continue until 1960 but they are arranged by port of arrival and there are no name indexes. There are also several earlier series of records that might help, including certificates of aliens arriving in the UK between 1836 and 1852, arranged by port of arrival. Each certificate gives the individual's nationality, their profession, date of arrival, last country visited and signature. In addition there are incomplete lists of immigrants arriving from Europe between 1836 and 1869, drawn up by the master of the ship on which they arrived. All these records are at the National Archives, and there is more information about immigrants on the website **www.movinghere.org.uk**.

Most people can discover the country an ancestor came from but do not know from which province or town. Unfortunately this is a vital piece of information as, across most of Europe, registration systems are based on towns or districts not nationally as they are in England and Wales. However, we've listed some books that may help you. There are also several (mainly American) websites which can provide useful information – many are listed at **www.cyndislist.com**.

By far the greatest number of immigrants to England and Wales came from Scotland and, especially, Ireland. There is no record of their arrival, so it can be difficult to work out when they came and where they came from.

In general, Scottish genealogy is very different to that south of the border, largely because the records used are unique to Scotland. Three major sources of records are held by the General Register Office for Scotland: civil registration from 1855, the census between 1841 and 1901, and the old parish registers (OPRs) that begin in the sixteenth century and go up to the end of 1854, for the Church of Scotland. Some records have also have been digitised and can be consulted online at **www.scotlandspeople.gov.uk** for a fee. Wills and probate material is held by the National Archives of Scotland, where you can also find the registers of some other churches, land and tax records. Their website is at **www.nas.gov.uk**.

The biggest problem with Irish research is that so much was destroyed in a disastrous fire in 1922. In addition, there are relatively few parish records for the eighteenth century and before, particularly for the majority Catholic population who suffered a great deal of persecution for their beliefs. Civil registration (the system is similar to England's) began in 1864 except for non-Catholic marriages from 1845. Few census records survive before 1901; both the 1901 and 1911 censuses are available at the National Archives of Ireland in Dublin. The most important source unique to Ireland is Griffith's Valuation, compiled between 1846 and 1865, which is a comprehensive list of 1.25 million landowners and tenants. Copies of the Valuation are now on CD-Rom and can be consulted online at **www.ancestry.co.uk**.

Emigration

Generally the best place to start is in the country to which an ancestor emigrated as these records are likely to be much fuller, provided of course you have this information. Before 1914 the most important destination, by far, for British and Irish emigrants was America, so it seems sensible to start there. For example, passenger lists for ships arriving in the United States begin in 1819; their British equivalents for ships leaving our shores don't start until 1890. There are large numbers of books, and an increasing number of resources available on the internet or CD-Rom, which can make hunting down ancestors who sought a new life across the Atlantic or in Australasia much easier. The records of Ellis Island, the main port of entry to the USA and Canada, are available online for 1892–1924 at **www.ellisisland.org**. However, it wasn't uncommon for people to work for a few years in the USA then, when they had made their fortune or become homesick, return to their families in Britain – this may explain why somebody apparently disappears and then suddenly reappears years later. The 1880 Census of both the USA and Canada is available online at **www.familyresearch.com**.

In Britain, passenger lists begin in 1890 for ships whose destinations were outside Europe and the Mediterranean and finish in 1960. They list everybody in the party, their ages and occupations as well as their address in Britain. These records are at the National Archives. However, there are so many passenger returns you really need to know the port where your ancestors sailed from, the year and the month and the name of the ship.

There were some government schemes to encourage emigration, although, in general, few records survive. Perhaps the most interesting of these plans was the New Zealand Company who in the 1840s wanted to build an idealised British society in the untamed bush: there are detailed records of the applicants, together with reference and other notes at the National Archives. Lists of pauper emigrants sometimes appear in the collections of Poor Law Union correspondence in series MH12, also in the National Archives.

Monumental inscriptions

Monuments in the church and the headstones in the churchyard can supply considerable information of genealogical value. It is not unusual to discover information that cannot be found elsewhere: relationships, ages, dates of birth, occupations, residences, personal details and more. In addition, there are brasses, bells, lights, windows, benefactors' boards, pews, organs, lecterns and stained glass, all of which may have some memorial inscription, if only a name and a date, and these should never be overlooked. The earliest inscribed memorials date from the sixteenth century and are, naturally enough, for the wealthier inhabitants of the parish.

It is often possible to be able to construct a sizeable, although possibly speculative, family tree from a single monument. To find a mother, father and two or three children buried in the same plot and all appearing in the inscription on the gravestone is not rare. Even the simplest inscription can fill a gap in your family tree or help prove the relationship between two individuals. When a married daughter is buried with her parents, her change of name is recorded on the memorial. Evidence of migration from another parish or even county may be revealed in the inscription. And, when a family member is brought 'home' for burial, their new residence may be given.

Gravestones, such as these in Norwood Cemetery, can provide a wealth of information, such as names, dates and relationships.

Family history societies have given much time and energy to the recording of inscriptions of memorials of all types within their area. In 1978, the Federation of Family History Societies launched a project to transcribe all unrecorded inscriptions in England. It was an enormous project and it is yet to be completed. This is essential work because both time and the elements result in many monuments being lost each year. Vandalism and developers also add to the problem: as recently as 1986, graves in the churchyard of St Mary Totnes in Devon were vandalised with signs of black magic rituals; others were smashed. Copies of these monumental inscriptions (often abbreviated as MIs) are usually deposited in local record offices or libraries, and sometimes at the church itself. The Society of Genealogists also has a huge collection of these transcripts and indexes among its holdings.

Reading old gravestones can be a time-consuming business. You need to be very careful that you don't damage the stone or any lichen living on it, so soft brushes and plenty of tender loving care are required. Many stones are already in a very fragile condition and there is a real danger of the face completely disintegrating if you scrub away. If the inscription is difficult to read, come back an hour or two later, as the change in the position of the sun can often make a remarkable difference. Inscriptions are often much clearer when the sun is low and casting stronger shadows. You may have to be very patient and it may take some time to extract everything that is on the monument.

As with any sort of transcription, copy down everything that can be read, from 'Sacred to the memory of' or 'In memory of' at the top, to the religious or other inscription at the end. No abbreviations, no expansions and no guessing. Always ask permission from the responsible authority before attempting any 'cleaning'. And make quite certain before you start that no one else has already transcribed the inscriptions.

Churchyard plans

Many parishes have produced plans showing where burials took place in the churchyard, which can be an invaluable aid in discovering the position of surviving monuments. They can also reveal the position of lost stones or those whose inscriptions are now impossible to read. Annotations on these plans may even indicate which individuals were buried in the same grave and thus help prove family relationships.

Cemeteries

Before 1827 there were no public cemeteries in London, with the exception of Bunhill Fields on the edge of the City, which was a nonconformist burial ground. In the 1830s and 1840s it was realised that something had to be done about the overcrowding in churchyards in London and other large towns. Groups of financiers decided to purchase land outside the residential areas, on the outskirts of the metropolis in rural surroundings, and establish new cemeteries. The first, in 1827, was Kensal Green Cemetery run by the General Cemetery Company.

The South Metropolitan Cemetery, as just one example, came into being in the then hamlet of Norwood in Surrey in 1837. Provincial cemeteries were opened in Liverpool, Leeds and Sheffield in the late 1820s and 1830s; others followed. During the early 1850s, a number of Burial Acts authorised local authorities in London and elsewhere to purchase land for non-denominational burials in cemeteries. By 1945, most private ownership of burial grounds had come to an end; they had become uneconomic and vandalism seemed an insurmountable problem. Rapidly, they were taken over by the local borough authorities.

Registers survive for most cemeteries, which describe the plot where the deceased was buried, the date of burial and to whom the plot belonged. These registers can sometimes be found at local record offices, but they are often still with the local authority responsible for maintaining the cemetery. These burial registers are usually very similar to church burial registers, but often there will be separate grave registers listing all those interred in each grave – sometimes as many as six – with the name and address of the person who originally purchased the grave.

Cremations

The building of the great Victorian cemeteries had helped considerably to alleviate the problems of disease caused by the overcrowded churchyards in the great cites. The movement in favour of cremation was based on similar concerns. The Cremation Act of 1902 allowed any public burial authority to provide and maintain crematoria. Now, about two-thirds of all disposals are by cremation. The Registers of Cremation are kept at each crematorium and are very similar to the Burial Registers.

Page 11211

BURIALS in the Year 18 *96* in the SOUTH METROPOLITAN CEMETERY, established under Stat. 6 & 7 William IV., c. 129.

Name.	Abode.	When Buried.	Age.	By whom the Ceremony was performed.
Alphonse Charles Jacques Alexander Ruffer No. A18849	51 Crystal Palace Park Road Sydenham	1896 apl 8	Yrs 76	A. Wyrard
Alexander Donald Sinclair Gosnell No. A18850	Chios House Poynders Rd Clapham Park	1896 apl 8	Mos 7½	Hugh St Maur Willoughby
Joseph Turner Matthews No. A18851	"Stonebridge" Giggshill Thames Ditton	1896 apl 8	Yrs 54	Hugh St Maur Willoughby
Dorothy Ellen Cooper No. A18852	17 Mordaunt Street Stockwell	1896 apl 8	Mos 2	Hugh St Maur Willoughby
Dorothy Margaret Owens No. A18853	643 Wandsworth Rd Clapham	1896 apl 9	Mos 8	Hugh St Maur Willoughby
Frederick Henry Clarke No. A18854	114 Cross Street Clapham	1896 apl 9	Mos 10	Hugh St Maur Willoughby
Sophia Hartjen No. A18855	29 The Chase Clapham Common	1896 apl 9	Yrs 60	Joseph B A Donovan
Alice Grace Emma Breaden No. A18856	2 Linton Terrace W. Norwood	1896 apl 9	Yrs 17	Hugh St Maur Willoughby

An extract from the burial register of the South Metropolitan (now Norwood) Cemetery for 1896.

The Crematorium at St Johns in Woking.

Memorials to those cremated may be found in the garden of remembrance or elsewhere nearby. The only permanent form of memorial at the crematoria is an entry in the Book of Remembrance. Unlike the cremation registers, they are available for public inspection and can sometimes include information in addition to name and date of death, such as age, date of birth and any official position held.

Internees

At the outbreak of the First World War in August 1914, it is thought that there were some 60,000 people of German extraction living in Britain, many of them Jews. In the first month of the war, the authorities instructed that all Germans aged between 17 and 55 should be interned, and others were to be repatriated. The Aliens Registration Act, which had been rushed through Parliament in

August, required all aliens to register with the local police. These aliens were then sought out and arrested. By late September approximately 10,000 alien civilians were in custody, but as the system was under enormous strain the process was suspended. Some records of alien families may survive within police records held locally, possibly in a county or local record office.

Where these alien internees were to be held was the major problem, Olympia in London and disused liners on the Thames were early solutions. However, the Isle of Man was soon concentrated upon as the best solution, commencing with Cunningham's Young Men's Holiday Camp, to be followed by the Territorial Army base at Knockaloe. When the War ended in November 1918, there were 24,450 men interned at Knockaloe.

Surprisingly, little survives in the way of records of First World War internees. The records of the Prisoners of War Information Bureau were destroyed by enemy action in 1940, and at the Public Record Office there are only a few records and none on the Isle of Man itself. Two specimen lists of German servicemen interned in 1915 and 1916 survive (WO 900/45-46) and there are other miscellaneous lists in WO 45 and 144. The International Committee of the Red Cross in Geneva holds an incomplete list of all known prisoners of war and internees of all nationalities. Their address is 19 Avenue de la Paix, Geneva CH-1202, Switzerland – an hourly fee is charged. The Religious Society of Friends, Friends House, Euston Road, London NW1 2BJ holds some material on internment camps.

Newspaper pictures showing First World War internees.

During the Second World War, a similar situation applied. Camps were again set up on the Isle of Man – where full records survive at the Isle of Man National Library, Manx Museum, Douglas IM1 3LY. Cards for individual enemy aliens between 1939 and 1947 are at the National Archives in HO 396.

Evacuees

As early as 1934, the government had been making plans for the evacuation of all children from Britain's large cities, should there be a war. Areas of the country were divided into three categories: evacuation (urban areas where heaving bombing was anticipated); neutral (areas that would neither send nor receive evacuees); and reception (rural areas where evacuees would be sent). During the Munich crisis in 1938, evacuation nearly took place but was abandoned when war was avoided. Several days before the outbreak of war in September 1939, it was decided to start moving people from the cities to the designated reception areas. This included 827,000 schoolchildren, 524,000 mothers and children under five, 13,000 expectant mothers, 103,000 teachers and 7,000 disabled people. In all, some 1.5 million children and adults were moved within three days, including 600,000 from London. This was still only half of the three million that the government had hoped would move. When the expected bombing failed to take place in 1939, doubts were raised as to whether the right decision had been made. By January 1940, an estimated one million evacuees had returned home. This was mainly due to the lack of any bombing, but homesickness, bad relationships between the evacuees and the foster homes, and the loneliness encountered by the mothers were also factors.

In May 1940, following the invasion of France, children who had been sent to the Kent, Sussex and East Anglian coastal areas were transferred to South Wales. By the end of July, almost 40 per cent of the population of Kent's coastal towns, and almost 50 per cent of East Anglia's had moved to safer regions of the country. Then, within a few weeks of the commencement of bombing by the Luftwaffe in July 1940, a further 213,000 unaccompanied children were evacuated from the large industrial cities. The government had set up a Children's Oversees Reception Board, which would arrange to send children to the USA, Canada and Australia. Within

A Second World War poster encouraging women to join the WVS to help with the organisation of evacuees.

a few months, almost a quarter of a million were registered with the scheme. However, when 73 children lost their lives when the *City of Benares* was sunk by a German torpedo in September 1940, the oversees evacuation programme was brought to a halt. In the same month, the Germans began to concentrate on bombing London, Liverpool, Birmingham, Plymouth, Coventry and other major cities. By December 1941, over 1,250,000 children had been moved out of these danger areas. Many children spent several years on farms miles away from their homes, and the National Farm Surveys (which are at the National Archives in MAF 65) taken during the period of the Second World War can give an insight as to conditions on individual farms.

Most children were evacuated through their schools: sometimes, entire schools moved, together with their teachers and helpers. It is therefore mainly education records where the family historian will find evidence of their parents' or grandparents' experience of evacuation. However, some children did not move with their own schools; or they returned home unofficially and may have been evacuated several times; and may have moved several times as reception areas became unsafe. Record-keeping therefore became extremely difficult, and most local authorities found it impossible to keep any sort of meaningful records about individuals. Although there are many records available relating to policy and other general matters, there is very little on individual children or schools. Logbooks of individual schools in London, from where most children were evacuated, do not often survive and where they do are subject to a 65-year closure. Those for schools in the reception areas may have fared better and these are the most likely place to find evidence of evacuated children.

CHAPTER 5

Military Records

War has played a major part in many families' lives during the nineteenth and twentieth centuries. During the two World Wars millions of men (and some women) enlisted in the armed forces, and not a few lost their lives in the service of their country.

Before you begin researching an ancestor's military career you need to know which service they were with (Army, Royal Navy or, after 1 April 1918, Royal Air Force) and approximately when they served. It is important to work out whether they were an officer (about 10 per cent of the total) or an ordinary soldier, rating or airman, as the records are very different. It is easy to check whether a man was an officer as they all appear in the official *Army, Navy* and *Air Force Lists.* Ideally you should also know which unit he served with, usually a regiment in the army, ship(s) in the navy and squadron in the RAF.

Two types of medal were awarded to servicemen. Campaign medals were given to all men who served in a particular campaign or theatre of operations – the first such medals were given to veterans of the Battle of Waterloo. You can normally find whether your ancestor was entitled to such a medal by looking at the medal rolls at the National Archives. Gallantry medals were generally awarded for specific acts of heroism: the Victoria Cross is the most prestigious such medal. Often a citation was published, which described the reason why the medal was awarded. They can be found in the *London Gazette,* but many have been published. Fully indexed copies of the *London Gazette* can be found online at **www.gazettes-online.co.uk** or at the National Archives and other large reference libraries.

The most important genealogical records are the service records which are at the National Archives, although documents for men who left the services after about 1920 are still with the Ministry of Defence. Other records you might use at the NA are muster, medal and casualty rolls, war diaries and logbooks, and reports and maps. Using these records it is possible to build up a detailed picture of your ancestor's career in the forces and the campaigns in which he was involved.

Over the years, many books have been published which contain lists of servicemen (particularly officers) who have either won a medal or died in action (known as rolls of honour), as they often contain extra biographical information. The Society of Genealogists, the Imperial War Museum and the National Archives libraries have large numbers of these books.

Finding out more

The vast majority of records you might use in the course of your research are with the National Archives, which are explored in detail on pages 56–57. However, there are a number of other museums which may well have records about your ancestor, the unit he served in and the battles and campaigns in which he fought. There is also a network of smaller museums for individual units or branches, many of which also maintain archives. Generally, regimental museums have little about individual soldiers, especially other ranks, although there are exceptions. The Essex Regiment Museum in Chelmsford is building up a detailed database of men who served with the regiment. These museums are listed in Terence and Shirley Wise's *A Guide to Military Museums and Other Places of Military Interest* or online at **www.armymuseums.org.uk**.

Commonwealth War Graves Commission

At its headquarters in Maidenhead, Berkshire, the Commonwealth War Graves Commission (CWGC) has details of all service personnel who died during the two World Wars and British civilians who died as a consequence of the Second World War.

The duties of the Commonwealth War Graves Commission is to mark and maintain the graves of the members of the forces from the Commonwealth who died in the First and Second World Wars, to build and maintain memorials to those who have no known grave, and to keep records and registers, including those of civilians who were killed during the Second World War. The work was founded on principles which have remained unaltered; that each of the dead should be commemorated individually by name on a headstone or

Reichswald Forest War Cemetery.

memorial; that the headstones should be uniform and that there should be no distinction made on account of military or civil rank, race or creed.

There are some 1.7 million commemorations for which the Commission is responsible in over 24,000 cemeteries. Copies of CWGC's memorial and cemetery registers are kept in the Printed Books Department of the Imperial War Museum.

The CWGC will accept postal enquiries for searches to be made in their sophisticated computerised Debt of Honour database. The database can also be searched online at **www.cwgc.org**. The information will tell you exactly where a man is buried, his unit, rank and service number and when he lost his life. It will sometimes include details of his family and where he was from.

Imperial War Museum
For those interested in twentieth-century conflict there is no better starting place than the Imperial War Museum in London. The main strength of the collections is their coverage of British and

CWGC	**DEBT OF HONOUR REGISTER**	
COMMONWEALTH WAR GRAVES COMMISSION	In Memory of	
	H D GRANDY	
	Private	
	36765	
	1st Bn., East Lancashire Regiment	
	who died on	
	Thursday 22 August 1918 . Age 20 .	
Latest News		
The Task	Additional Information:	Son of Thomas Robert and Jessie Grandy, of Undercroft House, Nelson St., Lower Broughton, Manchester.
Sir Fabian Ware		
Member Countries		
Commissioners	Cemetery:	AIRE COMMUNAL CEMETERYPas de Calais, France
Addresses	Grave or Reference Panel Number:	IV. B. 28.
Global Commitment	Location:	Aire is a town about 14 kilometres south-south-east of St. Omer. The Communal Cemetery is 0.75 kilometres north of the town, on the road to St. Omer and the four Commonwealth plots are on the east side.
Horticulture		
Architecture		
Publications		
Education	Historical Information:	From March 1915 to February 1918, Aire was a busy but peaceful centre used by Commonwealth forces as corps headquarters. The Highland Casualty Clearing Station was based there as was the 39th Stationary Hospital (from May 1917) and other medical units. Plot I contains burials from this period. The burials in plots II, III and IV (rows A to F) relate to the fighting of 1918, when the 54th Casualty Clearing Station came to Aire and the town was, for a while, within 13 kilometres of the German lines. The cemetery now contains 894 Commonwealth burials of the First World War and a few French and German war graves. There are also 21 Second War burials, mostly dating from the withdrawal to Dunkirk in May 1940. The Commonwealth plots were designed by Sir Herbert Baker.
Services & Links		
Home & Search		
	©2000-2002 The Commonwealth War Graves Commission. All Rights Reserved. Legal notices and terms of use	

You can search the comprehensive Debt of Honour database on the website of the Commonwealth War Graves Commission.

Commonwealth involvement in the two World Wars, but there is also an excellent collection of material on the post-Second World War period. The Museum's holdings cover the three services as well as the civilian experience of warfare. There are seven departments in the museum, any of which may hold material of interest. The Department of Printed Books houses what is possibly the most comprehensive collection of printed books on twentieth-century warfare with over 100,000 books, pamphlets and periodicals. In addition to the volumes of the several official histories produced by many of the nations involved, there is a comprehensive collection of regimental and unit histories, and service and prisoner-of-war periodicals.

The Department of Documents has a major collection of personal documents, including many unpublished diaries, poems, letters and memoirs. The Department of Photographs holds over six million prints, including photographs of units, ships, hospitals and numerous individuals, although usually of senior personnel. And the Department of Film and Video and of Sound includes 120 million feet of film, 6,500 hours of videotape and 32,000 hours of sound recording. These are supplemented by the Department of Art, which includes the majority of works commissioned under the official war artists scheme, and the Department of Exhibits and Firearms.

It is necessary to make an appointment to use any of the Museum's departments. Leaflets about using the Museum's resources for family history can be downloaded from their website **www.iwm.org.uk**.

National Army Museum

The National Army Museum, near Royal Chelsea Hospital, is dedicated to the history of the British Army since the seventeenth century. There are excellent displays on many aspects of the Army's history and the lives of soldiers. In addition there is a reading room with regimental histories and magazines, *Army Lists,* photographs, and the records of the Irish regiments which were disbanded on the creation of the Irish Free State in the early 1920s. Unfortunately, getting to use their reading room is a bureaucratic nightmare. Indexes to some holdings are now on the Access to Archives website **www.a2a.pro.gov.uk**.

National Maritime Museum

The National Maritime Museum (NMM) at Greenwich is best known for its collection of artefacts and historic relics, rather than as a resource for research. However, the Museum houses the Caird Library, the largest maritime reference library in the world. Most of the material held relates to the eighteenth century and before but there is nevertheless considerable information of interest to those researching more recent seamen, whether in the Merchant Service or Royal Navy. It is essential to make a reservation before visiting the Library, and a NMM Readers' Ticket is required.

The Historic Photographs collection dates back to the 1840s and now comprises some 250,000 negatives of maritime subjects, 500,000 prints and over 1,200 albums. Additionally there are 70,000 prints and drawings, 4,000 oil paintings and a million ships' plans. The catalogue of these images is available on the NMM website **www.nmm.ac.uk**. It is probable that they will have an illustration of any ship that an ancestor served on. The naval collection dates from the 1600s to the 1970s, and the merchant collection dates from the mid-nineteenth century to the 1960s.

One of the most important gateway websites for maritime research is run by the NMM at **www.port.nmm.ac.uk**, which includes links to naval organisations, societies, courses, discussion lists and museums.

Photographs of sailors sent home to loved ones in the Second World War usually had the ship's name or other insignia blacked out.

Royal Naval Museum

The Museum's Library in Portsmouth is of most use in tracing Royal Naval officers, rather than ratings, in the nineteenth and twentieth centuries. However, the Museum's library has recently begun a very ambitious *Naval Biographical Dictionary* project to record details of ratings and particularly officers.

Royal Air Force Museum

The museum, in Hendon, London holds many squadron histories, logbooks and photograph albums covering all RAF activities. There are also casualty records from the two World Wars. The collections cover the period before the formation of the RAF in 1918, with information on the Royal Flying Corps and the Royal Naval Air Service. In the Library can be found aviation magazines, which contain information about early aviators, and official air publications including training posters from the war. There are also extensive collections of photographs.

Liddle Collection

Also of importance is the Liddle Collection at the Brotherton Library, University of Leeds. This was founded over 30 years ago to collect and preserve first-hand individual experiences of the two World Wars. Included in the archive are original letters, diaries, official and personal papers and photographs, as well as written and tape-recorded recollections. They have a useful website at **www.leeds.ac.uk/library/spcoll/liddle**.

However, none of these collections includes any official personal service records or other official documentation. For these the researcher has to turn to the National Archives (or occasionally the Ministry of Defence). The exception to this is the Brigade of Guards and Household Cavalry, which generally holds its own personnel records.

Second World War

Service records for Army, Navy and Royal Air Force personnel are closed for 75 years. Therefore for anyone who served during the Second World War, his or her records are still held by the Ministry of Defence. Some information will be released by the MoD to the individual or to his or her next of kin for a fee (£25 in 2003). Army records are with the Ministry of Defence, Army Personnel Centre, Historic Disclosures, Mailpoint 400, Kentigern House, 65 Brown St, Glasgow G2 8EX. Records for naval officers are at Naval Correspondence, MoD Repository, Government Buildings, Bourne Avenue, Hayes, Middlesex UB3 1RS and ratings at Naval Pay and Pensions (Accounts), Centurion Building, Grange Rd, Gosport PO13 9XA. RAF records are held by the Ministry of Defence, PMA (CS) 2a2, Building 248a, RAF Innsworth, Gloucester GL3 1EZ.

Details of officers, of course, continue to appear in the *Army, Navy* and *Air Force Lists* and their dates of promotion are given. *Confidential Lists* were also published for the three services, which contain more information (including the unit a man served with) than the published list. The NA has a set. Tracing other ranks is more difficult – you may find appendices in RAF operation books and Army war diaries noting the transfer of personnel in and out of the unit, although by no means all survive.

On the ground floor at the Family Records Centre are indexes to service deaths from September 1939 to June 1948. These indexes are also available on microfiche elsewhere. You can use these indexes to order a death certificate in the normal way.

There is a roll of honour for Army personnel who died during the war at the NA. The roll covers those who died between 1 September 1939 and 31 December 1946. It is also now widely available on CD-Rom at libraries and record offices, including the National Archives and the Society of Genealogists. However the online records of the Commonwealth War Graves Commission, which were looked at earlier, are an easier starting source. Lists of Royal Naval personnel who died in action can be found in series ADM 104 at the NA.

Young men getting married in uniform can often narrow down the date and help you to identify the couple.

Probably the most interesting records you will use are the operational records, which for the Army and Royal Air Force comprise of daily summaries of activities. In the Army, these were called war diaries, which now are in several series of records arranged by theatre of operation. The diaries themselves detail the day-by-day happenings of the units concerned, sometimes in great detail. In addition the deaths of officers (and sometimes other ranks) are also usually given.

The equivalent in the Royal Air Force were the operation record books (usually referred to as ORBs), which are among the most detailed records available. They offer a fascinating insight into life in the RAF. Where appropriate, they will include details of every flight undertaken, together with details of aircraft and crew. Further information may be available in the combat reports, submitted after an enemy aircraft had been shot down, in series AIR 50, although these records are very patchy.

For the Royal Navy, the equivalent records to the Army war diaries, are the logbooks. However, these usually only report details of weather and position. More useful are the captains' reports made to the Admiralty: these cover specific operations and those of individual convoys, which can be found in series ADM 199.

First World War

At the outbreak of war the British Expeditionary Force was comprised of volunteer regular Army and territorial forces. During the early months of the war, hundreds of thousands of men flocked to the colours. They formed the 'New' or 'Kitchener's Army' (named after Lord Kitchener, the popular Secretary of State for War) and numbered more than three million officers and men by the end of 1915. However, as losses mounted, naturally enough voluntary enlistments quickly fell.

After considerable debate, conscription was introduced in March 1916. Initially this affected single men aged 18 to 41, but it was soon extended to include married men; and in April 1918 to those between 17 and 56. Conscription ended with the armistice in November 1918. Men could appeal against their call up, to military service tribunals. The vast majority of cases concerned employment (such as the last young man on a farm) or domestic arrangements (looking after elderly relations). Only a few related to conscientious objections against the war and warfare in general. Around 16,500 conscientious objectors obtained certificates from the military service tribunals exempting them from military service. Some were given total exemption but the majority were placed in non-combatant corps, put to work in labour camps run by the Home Office, or to other works of national importance. Those who failed with their appeal to a tribunal were sent to fight in France. If they continued with their objection, they were imprisoned, court-

Charles H Blake, the author's grandfather, in his First World War uniform.

martialled or worse. Nearly 1,300 conscientious objectors were imprisoned, 41 of whom were executed. Records of the courts-martial may be found at the National Archives (NA) in WO 90 and 213. Unfortunately, virtually all records of these tribunals have been destroyed, only the ones for Middlesex survive at the National Archives (series MH 47) and the odd item can be found at local record offices. However, tribunal sittings were covered fully by the local press, so you can usually find accounts in newspapers.

First World War service records: Army

For those who were members of the British Army there are a number of series of service records. If the individual was discharged before the end of 1920 (ordinary soldiers) or 1921/22 (officers), then the records, if they have survived, will be at the National Archives.

Nearly six million men enlisted as soldiers during the First World War but, regrettably, perhaps two-thirds of service papers for other ranks were destroyed during the Blitz. Those that survive have been microfilmed and are available at the National Archives in series WO 363 and WO 364: copies can also be ordered at local LDS family history centres. They are arranged in alphabetical order so are easy to use. As they cover men who were discharged or died in the period 1914 to 1920, they can include men who enlisted long before the start of the war, perhaps as early as 1892. The contents of each man's file varies considerably, but they can tell you when a man enlisted and was discharged, who his next of kin was, promotions through the ranks, and give details of units served in, and details of medical treatment received and any disciplinary charges. There may also be correspondence about pension or medal claims. What the records will not do is to tell you very much about any fighting he was engaged in – for this you will need to see the war diaries of the units he served with.

For commissioned officers (85 per cent of whose papers survive), there are two series of service papers, commonly called 'Territorial Officers' and 'Other Officers' in series WO 339 (with an index in WO 338) and WO 374. Both series include officers who served in the Royal Flying Corps (RFC). The officers' service files vary enormously in size and content, from a few sheets to many dozen, and may include letters, affidavits, medical and medal

(For the Duration of the W...)

ATTESTATION

No... Name *Blake* ...

142406 Questions to be put to the B...

1. What is your Name?
2. What is your full Address?
3. Are you a British Subject?
4. What is your Age?
5. What is your Trade or Calling?
6. Are you Married?
7. Have you ever served in any branch of His... Forces, Naval or Military, if so, which?
8. Are you willing to be vaccinated or re-vaccinated?
9. Are you willing to be enlisted for General Service?
10. Did you receive a Notice, and do you understand its meaning, and who gave it to you?

1. ...
2. 35 ...
3. *yes*
4. 25 Years. 309 Months
5. *Greengrocer*
6. *yes*
7. No.
8. *yes*
9. *yes*
10. *yes* { Name ... Corps ...

11. Are you willing to serve upon the following conditions provided His Majesty should so long require your services? For the Duration of the War, at ... of which you will be discharged with all convenient speed. You will be required ... serve for one day with the Colours and the remainder of the period in the Army Reserve ... in accordance with the provisions of the Royal Warrant dated 20th Oct., 1915, until such time as you may be called up by order of the Army Council. If employed with Hospitals, Depots of Mounted Units, or as a Clerk, etc., you may be retained after the termination of hostilities until your services can ... but such retention shall in no case exceed six months.

11. ...

I, *Charles Henry Blake* do solemnly declare that the above answ... the above questions are true, and that I am willing to fulfil the engagements made.

Charles H Blake SIGNATUR...

758 Coy Signature

OATH TO BE TAKEN BY RECRUIT ON ATTESTATION.

Charles Henry B... ...swear by ... faithful and bear true Allegiance to His Majesty King George ... His Heirs, ... and faithfully defend His Majesty, His ... and Suc... ...loyalty against all enemies, and will observe and obey all orders of His Maje... His ... Generals and Officers set over me. So help me God.

CERTIFICATE OF MAGISTRATE OR ATTESTING OFFICER.

The Recruit above named was cautioned by me that if he made ... answer to any of the ... would be liable to be punished as provided in the Army Act.

The above questions were then read to the Recruit in my presence.

I have taken care that he understands each question, and that his ... has ... replied to, and the said Recruit has made and signed the declaration and taken ... on this 10th day of ... 191 5

Signature of the Justice

† Certificate of Approving Officer.

... Attestation of the above-named Recruit is correct, an... filled up...

The First World War army service papers for Charles H Blake; the poor condition is a result of enemy bombing during the Second World War. Even so, it provides some fascinating information.

details. For officers promoted from the ranks, their original attestation papers will probably be included.

If the records for your ancestor have been destroyed, then you will need to use the medal index cards as these provide a comprehensive listing of soldiers who served during the war. Officers and other ranks (including the RAF), some women and some civilians were all eligible for one or more campaign medals, provided they served overseas. In particular, they can tell you: rank, regimental number, unit served in, other medals awarded, date of discharge; the theatre of war in which they served; and the date they were sent overseas.

These cards are indexes to the campaign medals that were issued to Army and RAF officers and other ranks. The 1914 Star (often called the 'Mons Star') was for service in France and Belgium during the period 5 August to 22 November 1914. The 1914–15 Star was for service from 5 August 1914 to 31 December 1915 in other theatres of war; and for service in France and Belgium from 23 November 1914 to 31 December 1915. Much more common were the British War and Victory medals, which were awarded to both military and civilian personnel who served in any theatre of war between August 1914 and June 1919.

The index cards are on microfiche. The alphabetical sequence within each surname can be slightly confusing: all those with a single forename (or initial) come first; these are followed by all those with two forenames, and then by those who have three. However, as you may not know of the existence of a second or third name, or the second or third name was not used, you need to be careful when using this index.

First World War service records: Royal Navy

For those ratings who joined the Royal Navy up until 1923, the records are at the National Archives in series ADM 188. Service records for Royal Naval officers (up to about 1920) are in ADM 196, except for Royal Naval Air Service officers, which are in ADM 273. There is a card index to the records in the Research Enquiries Room at Kew. The naval equivalent to the medal index cards are in ADM 171.

First World War service records: Royal Air Force, Royal Flying Corps and the Royal Naval Air Service

The Royal Air Force was founded on 1 April 1918 out of the Royal Flying Corps (RFC) and the Royal Naval Air Service (RNAS). Service records of those who died or were discharged from the RFC or RNAS before 1 April 1918 will be amongst those of the Army or Royal Navy respectively. Any medals received will also be in the relevant campaign medal rolls. RAF officers' service records are in series AIR 76, with airmen's records in AIR 79 – both are available on microfiche in the Microfilm Reading Room. AIR 76 was filmed with alternate pages upside down – you have been warned!

Gallantry medals

In addition to the campaign medals, many men gained gallantry or Meritorious Service Medals, or were Mentioned in Despatches. The National Archives has various series of registers noting the award

First World War medals, badges and 'dog tag' for Charles H Blake.

of individual medals. The entries usually give a reference to the issue of the *London Gazette* in which the award was announced, although it reasonably uncommon for citations to be published. The *London Gazette,* together with the *Edinburgh Gazette* and the *Belfast Gazette,* is available at **www.gazettes-online.co.uk.**

First World War deaths

For those who fell, there are several series of published lists of names, in addition to the records at the Commonwealth War Graves Commission previously discussed. The most comprehensive is the official *Soldiers Who Died in the Great War.* Originally this was an 81-volume work, prepared by the government in the early 1920s. As well as the date of death, entries can include date and place of enlistment, next of kin, and place of death (normally 'F&F' for France and Flanders). All entries are now available on CD-Rom, which is searchable by name and regiment. The CD-Rom is now widely available and most local history libraries should have a copy. A series of books called *The Cross of Sacrifice* describes officers in each of the services. Photos and short biographies of Army and Navy personnel appear in *De Ruvigny's Roll of Honour.* Death certificates of those who died between 1914 and 1921 can be obtained from the Office of National Statistics, and there are

A poignant image of the devastating human cost of the First World War.

indexes to deaths on the ground floor at the Family Records Centre. Death certificates for those who died in hospitals or outside the immediate war zone in France and Belgium, 1914–20, can be found at the NA in series RG 35. They are arranged alphabetically, and although in French or Flemish can be very informative.

For Royal Naval and Royal Marine personnel who were wounded or died as a result of enemy action, 1914–19, there are registers in ADM 104, with separate indexes and burial places for all ranks in the War Graves Roll in ADM 242. The RAF Museum at Hendon has an incomplete set of record cards for RFC and RAF casualties.

Operations
In addition to the service records already described, the National Archives holds many official records relating to the War itself, including: minutes of Cabinet and cabinet committees, records of the Supreme War Council, military planning and reports of operations, intelligence, and orders of battle (indicating where every unit was at a given time).

Possibly the most important series of such records is the Official War Diaries or Intelligence Summaries. From 1907, army units of battalion size or larger on active service were required to keep a daily record of all significant events, together with other information such as details of operations, lists of casualties and maps. These diaries are the most important source for discovering the deployment and other detailed information for every unit. There are no diaries for the campaign in South West Africa 1914–15, but included are military missions and armies of occupation. These records are in series WO 95. There is an index to battalions arranged by regiment, which will tell you where to look for the diary in the class list. If you have difficulties in locating a unit (this is not unusual), then staff will help.

The amount of detail in any particular diary depends on numerous factors, from the enthusiasm of the adjutant or junior officer responsible for completing them, to time available, which depended on the circumstances at that time. They can at times be difficult to read, partly because they were written in pencil and sometimes in a great hurry. They were also heavily abbreviated, so it can occasionally be difficult to work out what was going on.

It is unusual for individuals to be mentioned by name, especially other ranks. Officers are named only when they became a casualty

*Snapshots of wartime life for soldiers can help to paint a picture of your
ancestors, although they are often very difficult to date or locate accurately.*

or when posted elsewhere or sent home for training. However, this
lack of names is not necessarily important – knowing that your
ancestor was in that unit is sufficient for his service to be traced
through the period of the war. Should he have been awarded a
gallantry medal or mentioned in despatches, then the details of the
events surrounding the award can be discovered even when the
individual is not mentioned by name.

Trench maps can also provide a fascinating insight as to where an
individual soldier may have served much of his time. Sets are to be
found both at the National Archives and the Imperial War Museum.
A number of the Museum's maps have recently been published on
CD-Rom by the Naval and Military Press, **www.naval-military-
press.co.uk**.

Royal Navy operational records are not easy to use. They are
almost all to be found in series ADM 137, with some material in
ADM 116 and ADM 1. Almost all operational records for the RFC,
RNAS and RAF are in AIR 1 – look out for squadron operational
record books, which were the equivalent of war diaries. AIR 1 also
includes combat reports for enemy planes shot down and oddities
such as lists of pilots' belongings.

The nineteenth century and before

During the eighteenth and nineteenth centuries, tens of thousands of men served their country in either the Army or the Royal Navy. Even so, Britain's armed services have always been comparatively small. At the end of the nineteenth century, when Britain's imperial power was at it height, the total of all officers and men serving in the Army and Navy was a little short of 300,000. Again the National Archives is the main source of information, with some material at the National Army Museum in Chelsea. Records of men who served in the East India Company's armies until 1858 and in the Indian Army are held at the India Office Library and Records at the British Library.

On the ground floor at the Family Records Centre are several series of registers relating to Army personnel, including the Regimental Returns (1761–1924), Chaplains' Returns (1796–1880) and Army Registers (1881–1955). There are also records of deaths in South Africa 1899–1902.

For officers, the first records that should be checked are the official *Army* and *Navy Lists,* which begin in the early eighteenth century. The NA has almost a complete set, and incomplete runs can be found at the Society of Genealogists and other large libraries. For the Army, there is also the unofficial *Hart's Army List,* which was published between 1839 and 1915, which often includes biographical material not found in the official *List.* Once an officer has been discovered in a particular volume, his career in the Army or Navy can be traced back or forwards until the first and last entry is reached. An important date to note is when the officer was first appointed as a lieutenant as both Army and Navy can have significant records relating to this appointment.

For both services there are officers' service records. For the Army these are in two series: those produced by the regiment, commencing in 1764, and those produced by the War Office, from 1809. There is a single card index to both these series in the Research Enquiries Room at Kew. Royal Naval officers' service records begin in 1840 with some retrospective entries. There are several published biographies for naval officers, including *A Naval Biographical Dictionary* by WR O'Byrne, and *Royal Naval Biography* by J Marshall. Additionally, *Commissioned Sea Officers in the Royal Navy, 1660–1815* gives brief details of most officers – copies of these books are in the Library at Kew and at the Society of Genealogists. A number have also been reprinted by the Naval and Military Press and other publishers.

Commander in Chiefs' Memoranda, 1793–1871 (in series WO 30) can include much useful genealogical information surrounding the sale and purchase of commissions, particularly cadetships and lieutenancies. In the Navy, Lieutenants' Passing Certificates from 1691 can include details of previous service and other personal information in ADM 13 and ADM 107. There is an index to these records. Similar passing certificates also exist for captains, gunners, masters, pursers and paymasters.

For ordinary seamen and soldiers there are service records and musters. Service records for soldiers survive from 1756, but are almost exclusively only for those who were discharged to pension and can be found in WO 97, with many earlier records in WO 121. There is a computerised index at the NA to these records before 1854, which is also available online on PROCAT. However, between 1854 and 1883 it is necessary to know the regiment that the soldier served in. After 1883 they are arranged in a single alphabetical sequence. An alternative source are musters rolls arranged by regiment, which list every man in the battalion month by month. They date from the mid-eighteenth century up to 1898, although records for some units end in 1878 or earlier.

Before 1853, ordinary seamen signed on for a single voyage. And at the end of it, after a few weeks or months, and occasionally years, they were discharged. Many sailors spent their career on a mixture of merchant and naval ships and it can be difficult to find very much about them. The major source here are the ships' musters and pay books. It is essential to know the name of the ship on which the sailor served. Although these musters are very detailed, it was not until 1796 that columns were added for the age of the sailor and his place of birth. There are no service records for ratings (ordinary seamen) until 1853 when Continuous Service Records were introduced. These records are available to 1923 in series ADM 139 (1853 to 1872); and then in ADM 188, although they are ranged by the branch a man served with (signalling, gunnery and so on) rather than in alphabetical order. From 1872 they include full service details, together with personal information including date and place of birth, and a physical description. There are good indexes to both ADM 139 and 188.

Chapter 6

Growing Your Family Tree

Having read about the hard work, commitment and attention to detail that can be involved in tracing your ancestors, it's good to remind yourself regularly – as you pore over those precious and fading documents searching for the smallest clues – that the reason you became hooked in the first place was a desire to bring your ancestors alive. You are trying to learn about them as people, about how they lived their lives, who they loved and what mattered most to them. Piece by piece, you can build up an astonishingly detailed picture of what the world was like for them and how they lived their day-to-day lives. That's what family history is all about.

Whether you delve deep into the past or concentrate on just one or two generations is up to you. Even if this book only prompts you to record your own life, or perhaps that of your parents, you will be helping to keep alive for your descendants the essence of your personality and what it is like to live at the turn of the twenty-first century.

Life over the last hundred years has seen huge and astonishing changes, more than anything else because technological advance and development has proceeded at a rate that must have astounded even the scientists. It's hard to believe how different the lives of the two young girls in the

Edith Isaac.

Edith Isaac's great-grand-daughter, Melissa.

photographs – great-grandmother and great-grand-daughter – are likely to be; perhaps difficult even to credit that they were about the same age when the photographs were taken.

When Edith Isaac was turning 16 in 1908, Edward VII was still on the throne, the British Empire was one of the most powerful in the world, and most of the crowned heads of Europe were part of the extended family of the late Queen Victoria. Married just before the First World War, Edith saw her husband serve in the Great War and her sons fight in the Second World War. While she saw the advent of electricity in the home, labour-saving gadgets were few, work was scarce through the Depression, there was no welfare state, and her youngest son's four-year stay in hospital suffering from the respiratory disease tuberculosis was not that unusual.

As her great-grand-daughter, Melissa, turns 18, her world is one of opportunities that Edith could never have dreamed of. She can vote; she enjoys equality in education and in the workplace; contraception is freely available; world travel is commonplace; technology is ubiquitous – computers, mobile phones, electronic gadgets, instant communication are all taken for granted; we have seen photographs of distant planets of the solar system and microscopic organisms, and it is already more than three decades since men walked on the moon.

Personalising the facts you discover in this way can be a great encouragement to your researches, and help to remind you that – even if you only manage to gather a small amount of information on your immediate family – it could be immensely valuable to your great-grandchildren when they want to learn about their ancestors.

Suggested Questions to Ask When Compiling a Life Story

Once you start delving into your family's past, you will soon realise that there is a wealth of information readily available before you even start your research in libraries, record offices or on the internet. Only if you record information properly, can it become a real part of history for your children and grandchildren. You may want to start by asking your elderly relatives if you can talk to them about their lives and what they remember, and you can use the following suggestions and ideas to inspire you on the sort of questions to ask. Jot down your own questions – you are bound to think of more as you read through the list.

You probably know from your own experience that sometimes your memory needs jogging before it can recall details from the past. Asking specific questions, and especially showing photographs or memorabilia, are very effective ways to encourage your parents, grandparents and relatives to recall events and circumstances in their past. Ask them for anecdotes about their life; they are often the most revealing of sources about what it was really like at the time. Don't forget to ask if they have any photographs or documents that you might be able to consult or copy for your records.

Of course, the same questions are just as appropriate if you want to start with what you know best – your own life story. You are in a unique position to go into detail about your own life, and collect documents and specific information that will save your descendants a huge amount of work.

Remember to record and store all the information you gather carefully in a form that you can add to and develop gradually as your research progresses. You can use Appendix B to record your information, or compile your own record forms. A computer record is the easiest to update, but do remember to keep back-up copies on both disk and hard copy.

Personal

What is your full name?

Do you have any nicknames by which you are, or were, known?

Where did they originate?

When and where were you born?

Parents

What were your parents' full names?

When and where were they born?

When and where did they get married?

Can you describe your father?

What did he do for a living?

Did he serve in the armed forces?

What was the most remarkable thing about him?

Can you describe your mother?

What did she do for a living?

What was the most remarkable thing about her?

When and where did they die?

Siblings

Do you have any brothers and sisters?

What are their names?

When and where were they born?

Do you remember when any of them were born?

What do you most remember about them?

When and whom did they marry?

What do they do for a living?

Where do they live?

Are they still alive? If not, when did they die?

Childhood

What is your earliest memory?

What do you remember about life at home when you were small?

What were your favourite childhood games?

Where did you play?

Who were your best friends?

What can you remember about your clothes?

Did you get any pocket money?

How much pocket money did you receive?

What were your favourite sweets?

Did you go on family outings?

Did you go away on holiday?

When and where was your favourite holiday?

Do you remember any special family traditions?

Where did you spend Christmas?

What did you do on your birthday?

What sort of presents did you receive?

Home

Where did you live as a child?

What was your house like?

How many people lived in the house?

What sort of lighting did you have?

Did you have to help around the house?

What were your household chores?

Where did your mother do the shopping?

What were your neighbours like?

What was the neighbourhood like?

Where else have you lived?

Education

What was the name of your primary school?

When did you start and leave that school?

How did you get to school?

Who were your best friends at school?

Do you remember your teachers?

What was the name of your secondary school?

When did you attend that school?

Did you wear a uniform?

What was your uniform like?

What were your favourite subjects?

What is your best memory of school?

Did you pass any exams or win any prizes?

Who were your best friends there?

What were your teachers like?

Did you go to college or university?

Where and when did you attend further education?

What did you study?

Did you remain in touch with your friends?

Work

What was your first job and when did you start?

Can you remember your first day?

How much did you earn when you started?

What were your responsibilities?

What did you most like about your job?

What did you most dislike about your job?

How did you travel to work?

What other jobs have you done?

What companies have you worked for?

Who were your closest colleagues and friends?

Did you serve in the armed forces?

When did you retire?

Family

What is your spouse's name?

When and where was he/she born?

When and where did you meet him/her?

When and where did you get married?

What was the most memorable thing about your wedding?

Who was the best man?

Who were the bridesmaids?

What did you wear?

How many children do you have?

What are their names?

When and where were they born?

What are your most treasured memories of your children?

Where do they live now?

Are they married? If so, to whom?

Life experiences

What are your hobbies and interests?

What clubs or organisations have you belonged to?

What concerts, theatrical events or music festivals have you been to?

Have you ever attended any major sports events?

What are the most memorable events in your personal life?

If there is any event you would live over again, what is it?

Did you ever do anything outrageous?

Did you win any medals or awards?

Have you travelled abroad?

What are the most memorable national or international events in your lifetime?

What would you say has changed most during your lifetime?

Have you met any famous people? If so who, when and where?

Grandparents

Looking even further back, do you remember your maternal and paternal grandparents?

What were their names?

Can you describe them?

Do you know when and where they were born?

Do you know when and where they married?

How many children did they have?

Did all the children survive?

Where did they live?

What was their house like?

What type of work did they do?

Where did they work?

Did your grandfathers serve in the armed forces?

Do you know when and where they died?

Did they ever talk to you about their childhood?

Did they tell you anything about their own parents or grandparents?

Other relatives

Do you remember anything about your aunts and uncles?

Do you remember anything about your cousins?

What other relations can you remember?

Appendix B

Family Records

Use the following pages to make a note of as much information as you can about yourself and the people in your family. You can photocopy the pages for your personal use and fill them in, or develop your own record forms on hard copy or on a computer.

The more information you have, of course, the better, but don't worry if there are blank spaces. We all have to start somewhere. You may find that you know more about an individual than you think you do. The more questions you ask of the various members of your family, the quicker you will be able to fill in the gaps.

Personal

Full name
Nicknames, with origin
Where did they originate?
Date of birth
Place of birth
Relationship to you

Parents

Father's name
Mother's name
Father's date and place of birth
Mother's date and place of birth
Date and place of parents' marriage

Parents (cont.)

Description of father
Father's occupation
Details of father's military service
Remarkable features of father
Description of mother
Mother's occupation
Remarkable features of mother
Date and place of father's death
Date and place of mother's death

Siblings

Name and date of birth of   eldest sibling
Description or memories
Occupation
Address
Date and place of marriage
Name of spouse
Date and place of death
Name and date of birth of   sibling 2
Description or memories
Occupation
Address
Date and place of marriage

Siblings (cont.)

Name of spouse
Date and place of death
Name and date of birth of sibling 3
Description or memories
Occupation
Address
Date and place of marriage
Name of spouse
Date and place of death
Name and date of birth of sibling 4
Description or memories
Occupation
Address
Date and place of marriage
Name of spouse
Date and place of death
Other family memories

Childhood

Earliest memory
Memories of home life
Favourite childhood games
Best friends
Clothes
Pocket money
Favourite sweets
Family outings
Family holidays
Favourite holiday
Family traditions
Christmas traditions
Birthday traditions
Birthday presents

Home

Childhood address
Description of the house
People living in the house
Lighting
Household chores
Local shops
Neighbours
Other addresses and dates

Education

Primary school name and address	
Dates attended	
Travel arrangements	
Best friends	
Teachers	
Secondary school name and address	
Dates attended	
Uniform	
Favourite subjects	
Fondest memory	
Qualifications or awards	
Best friends	
Teachers	
Further education establishments	
Dates attended	
Course of study	
Friends	
Other school memories	

Work

Date and place of first job
Memories of first day
Starting salary
Responsibilities
Memories of the job
Travel arrangements
Other jobs with dates
Companies
Colleagues and friends
Details of military service
Details of retirement
Other work memories or details

Family

Full name of spouse
Date and place of birth
Circumstances of meeting
Date and place of wedding
Wedding memories
Best man
Bridesmaids
Wedding outfits
Name and date and place of birth of eldest child
Name and date and place of birth of child 2
Name and date and place of birth of child 3
Name and date and place of birth of child 4
Name and date and place of birth of child 5
Name and date and place of birth of child 6
Treasured memories
Current addresses
Details of marriages

Life experiences

Hobbies and interests
Clubs and organisations
Concerts, theatrical events or music festivals attended
Major sports events attended
Most memorable events
Event you would like to re-live
Outrageous actions
Medals and awards
Foreign travel
Memorable national or international events
Major changes
Details of meetings with famous people

Paternal grandparents

Name of paternal grandfather
Date and place of birth
Date and place of death
Description
Name of paternal grandmother
Date and place of birth
Date and place of death
Description
Date and place of marriage
Number of children
Address
Details of house
Occupations
Details of military service
Details of childhood
Memories or other information

Maternal grandparents

Name of maternal grandfather
Date and place of birth
Date and place of death
Description
Name of maternal grandmother
Date and place of birth
Date and place of death
Description
Date and place of marriage
Number of children
Address
Details of house
Occupations
Details of military service
Details of childhood
Memories or other information

Great-grandparents

Names

Any details

Other relatives

Memories of aunts and uncles

Memories of cousins

Memories of other relations

Other information

Checklist of Family Heirlooms

It is likely that you, or your family, will have a collection of heirlooms. These items can be a very valuable source for family history. You can use this form to compile an inventory for your family or just as an *aide memoire* to ensure you haven't forgotten a potential source. You may not have all the details – dates, for example – but record as much information as you can.

If you don't store everything together, you could keep a note of where to find the items. Of course, if you can set up a database of all this kind of information on your PC, it's much easier to keep up to date. Do remember to keep a back-up on floppy disk or CD-Rom.

Photographs – loose

Where taken	Date	People included

Photographs – in albums

Where taken	Date	People included

Postcards – loose

Location	Date	Details of picture or message

Postcards – in albums

Location	Date	Details of picture or message

Letters – personal

Written by	Date	Written to

Letters – official (including driving licences, national insurance)

Written by	Date	Written to

Wills

Will holder	Date	Beneficiaries or interesting details

School records such as reports, certificates

Name of person	Date	School

Military records such as discharge papers, medals

Name of person	Date	Details

Land records such as house deeds

Item	Date	Details

Cemetery records such as location of grave plots

Item	Date	Details

Miscellaneous records
such as swimming certificates, friendly society membership

Description	Date	Details

Family Bible

Description	Date	Details or inscriptions

Birth, marriage and death certificates

Certificate	Date	Name of person

Diaries

Diary holder	Date	Details

Newspaper cuttings

Newspaper	Date	Event described

Paintings or drawings

Artist	Date	Description

Silver, jewellery or furniture

Description	Date	Owner

Samplers

Embroiderer	Date	Description

Other items

Item	Date	Details

Census Dates and National Archive References

1841	6 June	HO 107		1881	3 April	RG 11
1851	30 March	HO 107		1891	5 April	RG 12
1861	7 April	RG 9		1901	31 March	RG 13
1871	2 April	RG 10				

Useful Publications

What's It All About?

General

Bevan A, *Tracing Your Ancestors in the Public Record Office* (6th edition PRO Publications 2002)

Blatchford R (ed.), *Family and Local History Handbook* (formerly the *Genealogical Services Directory Annual*)

Camp A J, *First Steps in Family History* (3rd edition, Society of Genealogists 1998)

Camp A J, *My Ancestor Came with the Conqueror: those who did and some of those who probably did not* (Society of Genealogists 1997)

Cole J and Titford J S, *Tracing your Family Tree* (2nd edition, Countryside Books 1997)

Colwell S, *Teach Yourself Tracing your Family History* (Teach Yourself 1997)

Fitzhugh T V H, *The Dictionary of Genealogy* (5th edition, A & C Black 1998)

Fowler S, *Joys of Family History* (PRO Publications 2001)

Gandy M, *An Introduction to Planning Research: Shortcuts in Family History* (FFHS 1993)

Gibson J and Hampson E, *Specialist Indexes for Family Historians* (FFHS 1998)

Herber M D, *Ancestral Trails: The Complete Guide to British Genealogy and Family History* (Sutton Publishing 2000)

Hey D, *The Oxford Companion to Local and Family History* (Oxford University Press 1998)

Hey D, *Oxford Guide to Family History* (2nd edition, Oxford University Press 2002)

Pelling G, *Beginning Your Family History* (7th edition FFHS 1998)

Raymond S and Gibson J, *English Genealogy: An Introductory Bibliography* (FFHS 1994)

Reader's Digest, *Explore Your Family's Past* (Reader's Digest 2000)

Rogers C D, *The Family Tree Detective* (3rd edition, Manchester University Press 1997)

Saul P (ed.), *The Family Historians' Enquire Within* (6th edition, FFHS 2003)

Titford J, *Succeeding in Family History: Helpful Hints and Time-saving Tips* (Countryside Books 2001)

Todd A, *Basic Sources for Family History* (3rd edition, Allen and Todd 1994)

Todd A, *Nuts And Bolts: Family History Problem Solving Through Family Reconstruction Techniques* (2nd edition, Allen and Todd 2000)

Unett J and Tanner A, *Making a Pedigree: An Introduction to Sources for Early Genealogy* (SoG 1997)

Using the Library of the Society of Genealogists (SoG, 1999)

British genealogical magazines

Ancestors, PO Box 38, Richmond TW9 4AJ, tel: 020 8876 3444, website: **www.pro.gov.uk/ancestorsmagazine**

Family History Monthly, 45 St Mary's Rd, London W5 5RQ, tel: 020 8579 1082

Family Tree Magazine, 61 Great Whyte, Ramsey, Huntingdon PE26 1HJ, tel: 01487 814050, **www.family-tree.co.uk**

Practical Family History, 61 Great Whyte, Ramsey, Huntingdon PE26 1HJ, tel: 01487 814050, **www.family-tree.co.uk**

Tracing living people

Amsden P, *Basic Approach to Making Contact With Relatives* (FFHS 1999)

Rogers C, *Tracing Missing Persons* (Manchester University Press 1986)

Wood T, *Basic Facts about Descendant Tracing* (FFHS 2002)

Names

Christmas BW, *Sources for One-name Studies and for Other Family Historians* (Guild of One-name Studies 1991)

Cottle B, *The Penguin Dictionary of Surnames* (2nd edition, Penguin 1978)

McKinley R A, *A History of British Surnames* (3rd edition, Longman 1990)

Palgrave D, *Forming a One-name Group* (4th edition, FFHS 1992)

Reaney P H, *A Dictionary of English Surnames* (3rd edition, Routledge 1997)

Redmonds G, *Surnames and Genealogy: a New Approach* (FFHS 2002)

Register of One-name Studies (18th edition, Guild of One-name Studies 2002)

Rogers C D, *The Surname Detective* (Manchester University Press 1995)

Titford J, *Searching for Surnames: A Practical Guide to their Meanings and Origins* (Countryside Books 2002)

Change of name

Josling J F, *Change of Name* (14th edition, Longman 1989)

Phillimore W P W and Fry E A, *An Index to Change of Name 1760–1901* (Longman 1910)

Genetics

Savin A, *DNA for Family Historians* (FFHS 2000)

Publications by family history societies

Hampson E, *Current Publications by Member Societies* (10th edition, FFHS 1999)

Perkins J, *Current Publications on Microfiche by Member Societies* (5th edition, FFHS 2002)

Starting Out

Contacting relations
Amsden P, *An Approach to Contacting Relatives* (FFHS 1999)

Heirlooms
Swinnerton I, *Sources for Family History in the Home* (FFHS 1995)

Photographs
Pols R, *Identifying Old Photographs* (FFHS 1998)

Pols R, *Family History from Old Photographs* (PRO Publications, 2002)

Steel D J and Taylor L (eds), *Family History in Focus* (Lutterworth 1984)

Who has been here before
Marshall G W, *The Genealogist's Guide* (London 1903)

Thompson T, *A Catalogue of British Family Histories* (Society of Genealogists 1980)

Whitmore J, *The Genealogical Guide* (Walford Bros 1953)

The British Isles Genealogical Register (The Big R) (FFHS 2000)

Genealogical Resources Directory (Australian Library of Genealogy annually)

Burke's Peerage and Baronetage

Burke's Landed Gentry of Great Britain and Ireland

Debrett's Peerage

Conducting Research

Finding archives and libraries
Codlin E M, *The ASLIB Directory of Information Sources in the United Kingdom* (ASLIB 1992)

Foster J and Sheppard J, *British Archives: a Guide to Archive Resources in the United Kingdom* (4th edition, Macmillan 2001)

Foster M, *A Comedy of Errors: the Marriage Records of England and Wales 1837–1900* (Michael Foster 1998)

Gibson J and Peskett P, *Record Offices: How to Find Them* (9th edition, FFHS 1998)

Harrold A, *Libraries in the United Kingdom and Republic of Ireland* (Library Association 1998)

Mortimer I, *Record Repositories in Great Britain* (11th edition, PRO Publications 1999)

Silverthorne E, *London Local Archives: A Directory of Local Authority Record Offices and Libraries* (4th edition, Guildhall Library 2000)

Titford J, *Writing and Publishing Your Family History* (FFHS 1996)

Wise T and S, *A Guide to Military Museums and Other Places of Military Interest* (10th edition, Terence Wise 2001).

The internet

Christian P, *Finding Genealogy on the Internet* (2nd edition, D Hawgood 2002)

Christian P, *The Genealogist's Internet* (PRO Publications 2001)

Hawgood D, *Family Search on the Internet* (D Hawgood 1999)

Hawgood D, *Internet for Genealogy* (2nd edition, D Hawgood 1999)

Hawgood D, *GENUKI: UK and Ireland Genealogy on the Internet* (D Hawgood 2000)

Peacock C, *The Good Web Guide* (2nd edition, The Good Guide 2002)

Raymond S A, *British Family History on CD* (FFHS 2001)

Raymond S A, *Family History on the Web: An Internet Directory for England and Wales: 2002–3 edition* (FFHS 2002)

Raymond S A, *Irish Family History on the Web* (FFHS 2002)

Raymond S A, *Scottish Family History on the Web: a Directory* (FFHS 2002)

Schaefer C K, *Instant Information on the Internet: A Genealogist's No-frills Guide to the British Isles* (Genealogical Publishing Co. 1999)

Online bookshops

Federation of Family History Societies: **www.familyhistorybooks.co.uk**

Genealogical Publications Company: **www.genealogical.com**

National Archives: **www.pro.gov.uk/bookshop**

Basic Sources

Civil registration

Collins A, *Basic Facts About Using the Family Records Centre* (FFHS 1997)

Langston B, *A Handbook to the Civil Registration Districts of England and Wales* (Brett Langston 2001)

Wiggins R, *Registration Districts* (Society of Genealogists 1998)

Wood I, *British Civil Registration* (2nd edition, FFHS 2000)

Wills

Collins A, *Using Wills After 1858 and First Avenue House* (FFHS 1998)

Cox J, *Wills Probates and Death Duty Registers* (FFHS 1993)

Gibson J and Churcill E, *Probate Jurisdictions: Where to Look for Wills* (5th edition FFHS 2002)

PRO, *Using Wills* (PRO Publications 2000)

Anglican and nonconformist registers

Gandy M, *English Nonconformity for Family Historians* (FFHS 1998)

Gandy M, *Tracing Catholic Ancestors* (PRO Publications 2000)

Gandy M, *Tracing Nonconformist Ancestors* (PRO Publications 2000)

Gibbens L, *Church Registers* (FFHS 1997)

Humphery-Smith C, *The Phillimore Atlas and Index of Parish Registers* (Phillimore 1995)

Palgrave Moore P, *Understanding the History and Records of Nonconformity* (3rd edition, Elvery Dowers Publications 1994)

Wenzerul R, *Jewish Ancestors? A Beginner's Guide to Jewish Genealogy in Great Britain* (2nd edition, Jewish Genealogical Society of Great Britain 2001)

Poor law records

Fowler S, *Using Poor Law Records* (PRO Publications 2001)

Gibson J, Rogers C and Webb C, *Poor Law Union Records* (4 vols, 2nd edition, FFHS 2001)

Census

Colwell S, *Family Records Centre: A Users' Guide* (2002 PRO Publications)

Gibson J and Hampson E, *Census Returns 1841–1891 in Microform: A Directory to Local Holdings in Great Britain* (6th edition, 1997 FFHS)

Lumas S, *Making Use of the Census* (4th edition, 2002 PRO Publications)

Occupations

Edwards C, *Railway Records: A Guide to Sources* (PRO Publications 2001)

Hogg P L, *Basic Facts about using Merchant Ship Records for Family Historians* (FFHS 1997)

Richards T, *Was your Grandfather a Railwayman? A Directory of Railway Archives for Family Historians* (4th edition, FFHS 2002)

Smith K, Watts C T and Watts M J, *Records of Merchant Shipping and Seamen* (PRO Publications 1998)

Tracing Your Family Tree: Merchant Seamen (Imperial War Museum 2000).

Watts, C T and M J, *My Ancestor Was a Merchant Seaman* (Society of Genealogists 2002)

Newspapers

Gibson J, Langston B and Smith B, *Local Newspapers 1750–1920: England and Wales, Channel Islands, Isle of Man* (2nd edition, FFHS 2002)

Collins A, *Basic Facts About Using Colindale and Other Newspaper Repositories* (FFHS 2001)

Maps

William Foot, *Maps for Family History* (PRO Publications 1994)

Immigration and emigration

Beare A, *Jewish Ancestors? A Guide to Jewish Genealogy in Latvia and Estonia* (FFHS 2001)

Davis B, *Irish Ancestry: A Beginners Guide* (3rd edition, FFHS 2001)

Fowler S, *Tracing Irish Ancestors* (PRO Publications 2001)

Fowler S, *Tracing Scottish Ancestors* (PRO Publications 2001)

Kershaw R, *Emigrants and Expats* (PRO Publications 2002)

Kershaw R and Pearsall M, *Immigrants and Aliens: A Guide to Sources* (PRO Publications 2000)

Maxwell I, *Tracing your Ancestors in Northern Ireland* (Stationery Office 1997)

Sinclair C, *Tracing your Scottish Ancestry* (2nd edition, Stationery Office 1997)

Sinclair C, *Jock Tamsin's Bairns: a History of the Records of the General Register Office for Scotland* (General Register Office for Scotland 2000)

Skyte T, *Jewish Ancestors? A Guide to Jewish Genealogy in Germany and Austria* (FFHS 2001)

Monumental inscriptions, churchyards, cemeteries
Bailey B, *Churchyards of England and Wales* (Robert Hale 1987)

Brooks C, *Mortal Remains, the History and Present State of the Victorian and Edwardian Cemetery* (Wheaton 1989)

Burgess F, *English Churchyard Memorials* (Lutterworth Press 1963)

Burman P and H Stapleton (eds), *The Churchyards Handbook* (Church House Publishing 1988)

Greenwood D, *Who's Buried Where in England* (Constable 1991)

Meller H, *London Cemeteries: An Illustrated Guide and Gazetteer* (3rd edition, Scolar 1994)

Pattison P, *Rayment's Notes on Recording Monumental Inscriptions* (4th edition, FFHS 1992)

Wolfston, P S, *Greater London Cemeteries and Crematoria* (4th edition, SoG 1997)

Military Records

Second World War
Cantwell J D, *The Second World War: a Guide to Documents in the Public Record Office* (HMSO 1993)

First World War
Beckett I F W, *The First World War: The Essential Guide to Sources at the National Archives* (PRO Publications 2002)

Fowler S, *Starting Out Tracing your First World War Ancestors* (Countryside Books 2003)

Holding N, *World War I Army Ancestry* (3rd edition, FFHS 1997)

Holding N, *More Sources of World War I Army Ancestry* (3rd edition, FFHS 1998)

Holding N and Swinnerton I, *The Location of British Army Records 1914–18* (4th edition, FFHS 1999)

Spencer W, *Army Service Records of the First World War* (3rd edition, PRO Publications 2001)

Swinnerton I, *Identifying your World War I Soldier from Badges and Photographs* (FFHS 2001)

Royal Air Force
Nesbitt R C, *The RAF In Camera: Archive Photographs from the Public Record Office* (Sutton Publishing 1995)

Spencer W, *Air Force Records for Family Historians* (PRO Publications 2000)

Royal Navy
Pappalardo B, *Tracing Your Naval Ancestors in the Public Records Office* (PRO Publications 2003)

Pappalardo B, *Using Naval Records* (PRO 2001)

Rodgers N A M, *Naval Records for Genealogists* (PRO Publications 1998)

Thomas G, *Records of the Royal Marines* (PRO Publications 1994)

Army
Fowler S and Spencer W, *Army Records for Family Historians* (2nd edition, PRO Publications 1998)

Holmes R, *Redcoat: The British Soldier in the Age of the Horse and the Musket* (HarperCollins 2001)

Isemonger P L and Scott C, *The Fighting Man: the Soldier at War from the Age of Napoleon to the Second World War* (Sutton 1998)

Roper M, *The Records of the War Office and Related Departments 1660–1964* (PRO Publications 1998)

Swinnerton I, *An Introduction to the British Army* (FFHS 1996)

Swinnerton I, *The British Army: its History, Tradition and Records* (FFHS 1996)

Useful Addresses

Borthwick Institute of Historical Research, Peaseholme Green, York YO1 2PW, tel: 01904 642315, website: **www.york.ac.uk/inst/bihr**

British Library, 96 Euston Road, London NW1 2DP, tel: 020 7412 7000, website: **www.bl.uk**

British Library Newspaper Library, Colindale Avenue London NW9 5HE, tel: 020 7412 7353, website: **www.bl.uk/collections/ newspapers.html**

BT Group Archives, Third Floor, Holborn Telephone Exchange, 268–270 High Holborn, London WC1V 7E, tel: 020 7492 8792, website: **www.btplc.com/Corporateinformation/BTArchives**

Catholic Central Library, Lancing Street, London NW1 1ND, tel: 020 7383 4333, website: **www.catholic-library.org.uk**

College of Arms, Queen Victoria Street, London EC4V 4BT, tel: 020 7248 2762, website: **www.college-of-arms.gov.uk**

Commonwealth War Graves Commission, 2 Marlow Road, Maidenhead, Berkshire SL6 7DX, tel: 01628 34221, website: **www.cwgc.org**

Family Records Centre, 1 Myddleton Street, London EC1R 1UW, tel: 020 8392 5300, website: **www.familyrecords.gov.uk**

Federation of Family History Societies, The Administrator, PO Box 2425, Coventry, Warwickshire CV5 6YX, website: **www.ffhs.org.uk**

General Register Office, PO Box 2, Southport PR8 2JD, tel: 0870 243 7788, website: **www.statistics.gov.uk**

General Register Office for Ireland, 8–11 Lombard St East, Dublin 2, Ireland, tel: 00353 1635 4000, website: **www.groireland.ie**

General Register Office for Scotland, New Register House, 3 West Register Street, Edinburgh EH1 3YT, tel: 0131 314 0380, website: **www.gro-scotland.gov.uk**

Guildhall Library, Aldermanbury, London EC2P 2EJ, tel: 020 7332 1863, website: **www.ihrinfo.ac.uk/gh**

Hyde Park Family History Centre: 64–68 Exhibition Road, London SW7 2PA, tel: 020 7589 8561, website: **www.familysearch.org**

Imperial War Museum, Lambeth Road, London SE1 6HZ, tel: 020 7416 5320, website: **www.iwm.org.uk**

Institute of Heraldic and Genealogical Studies, 79–82 Northgate, Canterbury, Kent CT1 1BA, tel: 01227 768664, website: **www.ihgs.ac.uk**

Liddell Collection, Special Collections, The Brotherton Library, University of Leeds Leeds LS2 9JT, tel: 0113 343 5518, website: **www.leeds.ac.uk/library/spcoll/liddle**

Modern Records Centre, University of Warwick Library, Coventry CV4 7AL, tel: 024 7652 4219, website: **www.warwick.ac.uk/ services/library/mrc**

National Army Museum, Royal Hospital Road, London SW3 4HT, tel: 020 7730 0717, website: **www.national-army-museum.ac.uk**

National Archives, Ruskin Avenue, Kew, Richmond, Surrey TW9 4DU, tel: 020 8392 5200, website: **www.pro.gov.uk**

National Archives of Scotland, HM General Register House, Edinburgh EH1 3YY, tel: 0131 535 1334, website: **www.nas.gov.uk**

National Archives of Ireland, Bishops St, Dublin 8, Ireland, tel: 00353 1407 2300, website: **www.nationalarchives.ie**

National Library of Wales, Aberystwyth, West Wales SY23 3BU, tel: 01970 632 800, website: **www.llgc.org.uk**

National Maritime Museum, Park Row, London SE10 9NF, tel: 020 8858 4422, website: **www.nmm.ac.uk**

National Register of Archives, National Archives, Quality House, Quality Court, Chancery Lane, London WC2A 1HP, tel: 020 7242 1198, website: **www.hmc.gov.uk**. The Register will be moving to the main National Archives building at Kew during 2003.

Principal Registry of the Family Division, First Avenue House, 44–49 High Holborn, London WC1V 6NP, tel: 020 7947 7000, website: **www.courtservice.gov.uk/fandl/prob_guidance.htm**

Public Record Office *see* National Archives

Public Record Office of Northern Ireland, 66 Balmoral Ave, Belfast BT9 6NY, tel: 028 9025 5905, website: **http://proni.nics.gov.uk**

RAF Museum, Grahame Park Way, London NW9 5LL, tel: 020 8205 2266, website: **www.rafmuseum.org.uk**

Royal Naval Museum, HM Naval Base (PP66), Portsmouth PO1 3NH, tel: 023 9272 7562, website: **www.royalnavalmuseum.org.uk**

Society of Genealogists, 14 Charterhouse Buildings, Goswell Road, London EC1M 7BA, tel: 020 7251 8799, website: **www.sog.org.uk**

The Postal Searches and Copies Department, York Probate Sub-registry, Castle Chambers, Clifford Street, York, YO1 9RG

Index